DANCE! ACCORDING TO THE SCRIPTURES

A Study Guide to
Starting and Maintaining
a *PROPHETIC* Dance Ministry

(c) Stine McDonald 2007

COPYRIGHT NOTICE:

Copyright law protects the material herein with the following amendments: The material herein, as given by the Lord, so intent is to help the body of Christ. Any reproduction to profit any other than the author is forbidden. The purchase of this book entitles the buyer to reproduce material herein for home or classroom use only – not for commercial resale. Reproduction of material herein for an entire School, Church, or District is prohibited. Any person's design to copy and use such for teaching to their whole Body of Believer's in Christ may do so only with the author's consent. No part of this book may be Reproduced (except as noted), stored in a retrieval system or transmitted in any form (mechanically, electronically, recording, etc.) without prior written consent of Publisher and /or Author.

First printing 2007

Printed in the United States

The Amplified Bible has been used by permission

ISBN 978-0-9791464-0-4

For Clandis, Robert and the SWATco Family

Table of Contents

ACKNOWLEDGMENTS   i
CREDITS   ii
INTRODUCTION   iii

Chapter 1

Commissioning - It's the Lord's Doing   1
Consecration and Separation   1
Write, Read, RUN with the Vision   3
Don't Rush the Vision   3
The Lord Will Name Your "Baby"   3
Develop a Mission Statement   5
Submit the Vision to Your Under-Shepherd   6
Don't Despise the Day of Small Things   7

Chapter 2

Search Out the Resources   8
Get Knowledge and Understanding   8
Be Skillful   8
Ask God for the Right Help   9

Chapter 3

The Divine Covering — Garments in Ministry   10
Our Garments Should Speak!   11
The Priestly Garment   17
The Anointing on the Garment   18
Who's Handling the Garment?   20

Chapter 4

Discernment is a Key — Things to Watch For   22
The Luciferian Spirit   22
Witchcraft   23
Competitiveness and Covetousness   24
Comparisons   24
Envy, Jealousy and Strife   25
The Great Rebellion!   25

Chapter 5

Are You Ready to Dance?!   26
Set Rehearsal Times and Guidelines   26
Don't Limit God!   27
Various Forms of Dance that God Uses   28
The Choreography   29
Prophetic Choreography   30
Flowing with the Psalmists & Musicians   31
It's Sacred, What We Do   31

Chapter 6

Exercises and Basic Dance   33
Breathing   37
Proper Alignment and Posture   37
Stretching   38

Five Basic Ballet Positions	39
Basic Ballet Terms and Demonstrations	46
Basic Laws that Govern Dance	67
C O N C L U S I O N	71
About the Author	76
Glossary Note	77
Glossary of Terms and Commentary	78
The Holy Spirit, Appendix – A	86
Scripture Appendix - B	88

Acknowledgements

To my Precious Holy Spirit, My Lord Jesus, My Redeemer, My Healer, My Deliverer and My Father God, Thank You for showing me how to push past the pain
to birth what you've given me.

Thank You Mom (Adele) for always making me believe I can do ANYTHING because you could always do ANYTHING.

Thank You Dad (Mac) for loving me…always!

Thank You Danny Stewart for the honor of raising a Great Man and for blessing me with Daniel, Taylin, Daya and Aidan!

Thank You Andrea and Lee Elliot for helping me through the most difficult times of my life and still returning my calls!

Thank You to my wonderful friend, Lynell, you are a beautiful picture of Jesus.

Credits

Artist Renderings
Isaiah Custard and Jeremiah Custard

Book Cover Concept
Stine McDonald

Dance Demonstrators
Kristopher Nobles and Tatiana Stewart

Editor
Julie Larson

Photography and Book Cover Graphic Design
Terri Griffin Photography, Los Angeles

Printing
Faith Printing, Franklin IL

Steps Ordered by God Publishing

INTRODUCTION

One of the first things God began to teach me years ago was the *integrity of His Word.* That was important for me because I had learned (like most) that people don't always do what they say — that's life! Since I didn't have a frame of reference, the Lord began to show me little by little over the years that *He is the God of His Word.* Since God has given us His Word in the form of the Scriptures, we can be assured that if we follow His prescription (before-written Word) on any subject, we know we have His Will in the matter and that Word is *Re-Liable.* By my definition, *Re-Liable* means we can lay down on His Word and be fully supported over and over again. He's liable or accountable for what He tells us, over and over again. He says that His Word "is a lamp unto our feet and a light unto our path" and he means that. As dance ministers, we must allow that Word to light our feet up in every area! **God doesn't do anything apart from His Word. He and His Word are one.**

[Referenced Scriptures: OLD TESTAMENT: NUMBERS 23:19. PSALM 119:105. ISAIAH 40:8, 55:11. JEREMIAH 1:11-12. NEW TESTAMENT: MARK 13:31. JOHN 1:1. 1 CORINTHIANS 15:3-4. 1 PETER 1:22-25.] See Scripture Appendix, page 90.

Let me Encourage Your Heart!

As we go along, please have your Bible open and be ready to look up *(and truly study)* each referenced Scripture, or refer to the Scripture Appendix at the end of this Study Guide. The words on these pages are those which I believe God has given me to write, but it's *His* Word, that will never change, *His* Divine Counsel, *His* Truth packed with Eternity that is going to breathe life into you, give you vision, speak destiny and complete Faith to your heart, it will renew your mind so you can SEE! It's **the Word** that does **the work**. The operative words in the title of this teaching are "According to the Scriptures," and the principles that are laid out can be applied to starting and maintaining just about anything at all! As you continue in this study, my prayer is that you would have a deeper and richer love for His Word, above all else. Okay... so now you know my ulterior motive for writing this book!

My further prayer for you as you go through this Manual is that God will give unto you the spirit of wisdom and revelation in the knowledge of Him, that He will FILL you with the knowledge of His Will in all wisdom and spiritual understanding, and that the Holy Spirit will take you on a glorious journey, teaching you exactly what you need for THIS season of your life and ministry. I pray that He would navigate you around, over, under or through any hindrance to laying hold to and doing what He's called **you** to do, and lastly, that you would be inspired and fired up to go forward, becoming an absolute threat to the enemy.

[**Referenced Scriptures**: NEW TESTAMENT: ROMANS 10:17. EPHESIANS 1:17-20. COLOSSIANS 1:9-10. 2 TIMOTHY 3:16-17. 1 JOHN 2:20-27.] *Are you ready with your Bible? Check out these Scriptures now!* ... or see Scripture Appendix, page 91.

What Did God Say?

The very first thing you want to prayerfully consider when starting a Dance Ministry is the answer to this all-important question: *"What did God say?"* Remember what your mom or dad (mostly mom) would say when you looked as though you would not carry out their requests? *"What Did I Say!!!"* When you heard those words, you would scramble to do what had been commanded because consequences to disobedience were soon coming! It is vitally important to keep [not only what He said but what He FIRST said] before us because believe me, it is E-A-S-Y to get off track. When we do get off track, we have to hear God say *"What Did I Say!!!* And we have to scramble back to the thing He said at the FIRST.

If we look at the principle of "firsts" in Genesis, the Book of Beginnings, we see a road map and are able to unearth nuggets of gold along the way relative to how things are started. **The very *FIRST* thing God did in creation was to MOVE.**

> *Okay all you dance ministers,* let's take a little "side bar" before reading on. The original Hebrew for the word "move" in Genesis 1, is *Rachaph*, which literally means "to brood" like a hen sitting on eggs. I always found it interesting that the word designating movement translates to mere sitting! Think about it — how does "to move" and "to sit" have the same meaning? The Holy Spirit, the Revealer of Truth, allowed me to see it this way: A mother hen sits on her eggs brooding, *why?* To bring maturity to what is inside the egg, right? Right! Scientifically we know that heat promotes maturity. In this case, heat is produced by the movement. But where is the movement coming from? The heart is pumping the blood…and the blood is *MOVING!* Selah, take a moment and let the Lord Speak a personal revelation about this… Alright, back to what God did and then said…

After He moved, He SPOKE. God generally speaks after He moves or is moved. That's why praise and worship is such an important part of our church service — there is an inhabitation of our praise that MOVES us to Him! *Then,* He speaks to us. Just the same way He prepared the earth to receive His Word by moving before He spoke; likewise, He moves on our hearts during worship, to prepare our hearts for His Word that comes through the Pastor or the speaker. He moves and then He speaks.

But wait a minute… what if God happens to be silent? Then what? Simple. If He has nothing to say, we have nothing to say. We must be silent or still as well, we follow His lead and until He gives specific direction, we must remain still. Until we get a leading Word or the path lit up, we shouldn't be moving forward as we will be in the dark. And why should we move in the dark when we have the illuminator, which is Jesus, Who is The Word, living on the inside of us. The entrance and unfolding of His Word giveth light and understanding (discernment and comprehension) to the simple. *Remember, Jesus did nothing on His own, He always had His Father's direction.*

God does nothing by chance or accident - it's ALL purposeful. For example, after God spoke light into existence, He NAMED it. When He named light, He called it "day," and we find that when God names something, that name is a prophetic command. In other words, "Day" has to "be lit up."

The Next thing God did in creation was APPROVE. He said, "It is good." You will know in your spirit that God is pleased, and there will be fruit or proof of it by His tangible presence and people will un-mistakenly be blessed. However, the greatest proof that God has approved a thing is the PEACE that is inside of you regardless of what people are saying or doing!

If at this point, you know that God has given you a "green light," for starting or maintaining a Dance Ministry, then you're on your way somewhere to make something wonderful happen with God, and He will confirm His Word with signs following. But don't forget: You are going to need to stand on the solid ground of what God has said when trouble comes, and trouble will come — **it's coming for the Word's sake**.

As we continue to look at the creative power of God's Word, I'm reminded of the account of the prophet Ezekiel in the 37th Chapter, when God asked him, "Can these bones live?" and the prophet very wisely responded, "Oh Lord God, Thou knowest." *Now that was the right answer.* God knows, and in His ultimate, infinite knowledge has declared the end from the beginning. The passage continues with God telling the prophet to **speak** to those very dry bones and for those bones to HEAR THE WORD OF THE LORD. I like God — He has us speaking to inanimate objects and they obey! (Anybody speaking to the mountain out there?! Are you commanding the Airways??!!) Yes, I love our God because when the prophet obeyed and spoke God's Words to the dry bones, God Himself went into action to do His part. (I like to call Him the God of *The Partnership*.) He began to wrap the bones with sinew and bring up the flesh and cover it with skin, and then He did the thing that He and only He can do: He BREATHED upon those bones and they didn't have any choice BUT TO LIVE! You just go ahead, God — *breathe* on us! If anything we do has life in it and it's fresh and inspirational and has impact, and — my personal favorite when expressing God's power — if there's any *efficaciousness* to it, it's because God has breathed on it. The key, however, is that God will breathe on it because it is *His Will.* It's His plan, not ours; His way, not ours; His timing, not ours — and our wonderful God is obligated to make His plan clear and plain. It's so important to allow God to be the initiator, igniter or starter in what we do and then look to Him to continue it. He is a Keeper (in so many different ways). He's the Author, the Chief Leader/Developer of our faith and faithfulness. Frankly, we can't initiate any life or action of life without Him because *ALL life comes from Him.*

So *seek Him* and find out if God is leading and directing you to dance before Him. Be certain it is not just because it may appear to have some popularity and everyone's jumping on the bandwagon; all of those will start with a blaze of glory but the fuse with soon burn out! Be sure it's God and be sure you're the one. We want some staying power in what we do. Is starting a dance ministry God's destiny for you? You may *want* to begin a dance ministry, but God may have someone else in mind to actually bring it to fruition. Be open to what the Lord is saying. One thing is for sure — if starting a dance ministry is **not** the thing YOU are to do, while seeking Him, He will surely make your personal path clear to you. Isaiah 48:17 (Amplified) says: "Thus says the Lord, your Redeemer, the Holy One of Israel; I am the Lord your God, who teaches you to profit, who leads you in the way that you should go." On the other hand, if you find that starting a dance ministry is like FIRE SHUT UP in your bones and it can't be dismissed, then I would recommend that you stay in prayer as you read on, and get ready because *it's gonna get hot from here!*

[Referenced Scriptures: OLD TESTAMENT: GENESIS 1-2. PSALMS 22:3, 46:10, 119:130 (AMPLIFIED), 127:1-2 (AMPLIFIED). ISAIAH 48:17 (AMPLIFIED). JEREMIAH 20:9. EZEKIEL 37:1-10. NEW TESTAMENT: MARK 4:14-20. JOHN 5:43, 6:63, 8:28, 10:30. REVELATIONS 3:15-16.] See Scripture Appendix, page 92.

Chapter 1

Commissioning-It's the Lord's Doing

When the Lord commissions you or sends you to do a task, a whole new level of dedication, sacrifice and work is required. Co-Mission is defined as follows: Co meaning "with", Mission meaning "something sent" and it has the same root as the word "Missile". Think of the Power with which a missile is launched. Also consider the different types of missiles; i.e., heat seeking. Lastly, consider the warhead on the missile and its design to take the enemy OUT! So God doesn't just send you, He sends you PACKING. Additionally, you never go alone, HE IS "with" you. He did say He'll never leave nor forsake you.

Consecration and Separation

You must spend some consecrated, separated time before the Lord — quiet times of fasting and prayer.[†] This will produce some real power in your life and ministry. You position yourself for God to remove the non-essentials. These non-essentials may be GOOD things but they may not be necessary for the season that you're in today. It produces a purging of "self." This is extremely necessary because "self" is of the "flesh" and the flesh doesn't have a clue what God is doing. In fact, the flesh is by its very nature *hostile* to God. There can be no revelation when we are "in the flesh." Once we rid ourselves of *ourselves*, we can take on Him.

When the Lord begins to take me to a new place in Him, I find that He often requires a quiet time of fasting and prayer so that my spiritual ear is opened and my spiritual neck is "un-stiffened." When the figurative neck is stiff, it means we are dense or dull of hearing and hard to get through to. To prepare for a new "season," we must be able to see things in a new and fresh way. It's very difficult to look at things in a new light if the neck won't allow the head, where the vision abides, to turn! When our vision is obscured by "baggage" or force of habit, God's plan for us becomes clouded and we can't see things the way He's showing it. We then tend to fly off on a tangent. We become presumptuous: *pre-* meaning "before," and *sum-* meaning "total or conclusion" — i.e., *we come to a conclusion before the time, before we have all the relevant information.* As human beings, we are the most presumptuous creatures in existence. We tend to think that we know what God is saying only to find out later that He had a different design all along. Of course He won't tell us everything — He is a God of Faith and requires that we simply trust in Him. However, there are certain things that we must know in order to cooperate with Him. *Okay, short prayer: "Lord, please keep us from presumptuous sins."*

[Referenced Scriptures: OLD TESTAMENT: PSALMS 19:13, 46:10, 118:23. NEW TESTAMENT: JOHN 3:30, 6:63. ROMANS 8:1-13. HEBREWS 11:6. REVELATION 2:29.]
See Scripture Appendix, page 95.

[†] It is advisable to consult a physician before starting any diet or exercise program.

Write, Read, RUN with the Vision

While spending that precious time with Him, God gives you Vision (you become a Visionary). He plants the Vision seed inside your heart, and you become pregnant with His Word. Much like Mary, when she yielded and agreed with God (He had His Way with her) for His Will for her by saying, "Be it unto me according to Thy Word." As your Vision unfolds to you or is revealed to you by the Lord, write it according to Habakkuk and make it plain upon tables (or writing tablets) so he may run that reads it. The word *write* in Habakkuk 2:2 means "to grave or write or record." In other words, dig deep or engrave what God says because it's *permanent* — you can **mark** His Words. Now, the first person that needs to run with the vision is you! You must keep the vision before you so you can remain constant in the race!

[**Referenced Scriptures**: OLD TESTAMENT: HABAKKUK 2:2-3. NEW TESTAMENT: LUKE 1:38.] See Scripture Appendix, page 96.

Don't Rush the Vision

Don't be in a hurry! Although sometimes there's a sense of urgency and God will require you to move speedily, you should never feel stressed or anxious. He is methodical and purposeful and will give you each step in the development process. You will find it is He who is developing the Ministry, but most importantly, He's developing YOU and your character as well along the way! He's proving you and stretching your faith because He's creating room for increase and greatness on the inside of you, so embrace it and enjoy the journey!...I know, easier said than done but faith without works is well, you know.

[**Referenced Scriptures**: OLD TESTAMENT: HABAKKUK 2:1-3, JAMES 2:26.] See Scripture Appendix, page 97.

The Lord Will Name Your "Baby"

The Lord will name your ministry. You see, the Father names the child, and in that name will be destiny. Ask God to give you

His name for the ministry He's given you. And it will be wrapped in His Word.

You will find His purpose for the ministry in that name because it will be prophetic.

My favorite definition of *prophetic* is very simple. It means "God Speaking" — before the time (only He knows our future) and to our "right now"...oh! We are back again to what God is Saying!!!. There is a theme here! The word "prophetic" is over-used in the Body of Christ, but it *is* so specifically significant in the ministry of Arts. God is speaking through the Arts like never before because people will not always hear the spoken word from the Pastor or speaker from the pulpit. Many have learned to plug up their spiritual ears (without their knowledge). Our God is using the visual, musical prophetic arts to otherwise engage people to see and hear His Word of Hope and Salvation.

A prophetic, timely and anointed ministry word from the Arts can change the atmosphere and prepare the hearts to receive the Word that is coming from the Pastor or speaker, so that the Word spoken can be engrafted like never before. **God uses us to make it EASIER for the speaker to deliver the Word God has given them.**

The name of my Ministry is "Steps Ordered by God." It is a specific, personal, prophetic Word from God, to me. It speaks to *my* Ministry's purpose whether it's steps of action, steps of faith, or steps in the choreography. The name that God will give *you* will speak the Vision to you over and over and will continually establish a path for you to pursue. It will also keep you on that path as each time the name is used, you'll be speaking the

Vision to your own heart and it will shape your choices. Faith comes by hearing, and hearing by the Word of God.

[**Referenced Scriptures**: OLD TESTAMENT: GENESIS 17:5, 35:18, ZECHARIAH 7:11. NEW TESTAMENT: LUKE 1:57-66. ROMANS 10:17. PHILIPPIANS 1:6. HEBREWS 12:2.] See Scripture Appendix, page 97.

Develop a Mission Statement

Once you have the name, you can then develop your Mission Statement by answering these questions: What primary objective has God given you to accomplish? What is the focus of your Ministry? To whom is your Ministry geared? How will your target audience benefit? What are the major activities in which you will engage to carry out your mission?

The mission of "Steps Ordered by God" Ministries is to **_teach God's Word_**. My Ministry's primary means of accomplishing this mission is through the arts; dance, drama, comedy, songs, scripts, literature, etc. No matter the arts vehicle I utilize, it's always a teaching tool on what God has said. My ministry also engages and encouraging others to do the same - I don't want to just dance, I pray that my dance teaches and preaches, then, through God's Word, I want to teach others how to teach others how to teach...you get the picture!

The steps that God has given me to carry out the vision are ORDERS not requests and they are orderly, I am not allowed to "skip a step". I tend to want to do that (it's my personality) so I'm reminded when I see "Steps Ordered by God" that He has pre-determined, established, arranged, orchestrated and ordained each step I must take in the teaching/preaching process. See, the name is constantly speaking vision and how to carry it out! The same can be said for others throughout history according to the Scriptures. For instance, when God gave Noah the plan for the Ark, it was very purposeful and patterned. When God gave David the plan for the House of God which He passed on to Solomon, the same was true — *and the same can be said for you!* The Lord will give you His Plan because He needs a man/woman here on the earth to work His Will. He will happily give you His Plan and place things in your heart so you can carry them out because He wants us to co-labor with Him!...but be forewarned, we are often tempted to feel as though we accomplish things in our own strength. We have this Treasure in an Earthen Vessel, and as such, we tend to think somehow WE get the work done on our own. The "Earthen" or "Earthly - Human" part of us wants to take over. The true "Treasure" is **in** us, not us! I can't stress enough the need for you to let Him do HIS work through you. We are merely transporters of and "sharers" in His Glory. He is so gracious!

[Referenced Scriptures: OLD TESTAMENT: GENESIS 6:13&17. 1 CHRONICLES 28:11-20. ZECHARIAH 4:6. NEW TESTAMENT: 2 CORINTHIANS 4:5-7. PHILIPPIANS 2:12-13 (AMPLIFIED). 1 THESSALONIANS 5:24.] See Scripture Appendix, page 98.

Submit the Vision to Your Under-Shepherd (Your Pastor)

In-house ministry: Start by consulting a visionary leader of your church, such as your pastor or arts ministry leader if that person is more accessible. The point is, go to the top (where your overseer or leader is) and share what's in your heart. All things being equal, there should be agreement with what God has given you and, as your overseer in the spirit, what God has shown them about you - the qualifier here is "all things being equal". Your experience and situation may be unique and require another strategy for submitting the vision - God will surely show you what to do. If there is a problem situation, follow the instructions of your Pastor and pray - God will move in the situation. God respects order and protocol. Protocol is a pre-determined system on how things are carried out.

Ministry Outside the House: If you're being led to start a Dance Ministry on your own, outside of your local church, you must still consult with your pastor because you will need a release and a covering from your under-shepherd (who is your pastor -- Jesus is the Good Shepherd). All things being equal.

God being a God of order and protocol requires us to respect authority. Submission is a powerful thing. By submitting your vision to your spiritual leader, you open yourself to a potential pool of God-given wisdom, as well as unique mentoring opportunities. It is, however, your *submissiveness* that means so much to God. We don't HAVE to submit, it is an act of our free will. But when we DO submit out of love and obedience, *oh my! ... that* is a turn-on for our wonderful God! Your submission places you under the covering that God has woven for you which provides direction, instruction and protection — all of which is very, very important! Lastly, the anointing (which you need) comes down from the top or leadership. Look at Psalm 133. When we are in order or alignment, we can expect to be anointed! It's the anointing that destroys the yoke of bondage; it is extremely valuable and must be protected at all costs. The anointing is defined as something that is "smeared on" or rubbed on.

[**Referenced Scriptures**: OLD TESTAMENT: PSALM 133:1-3. ISAIAH 10:27. NEW TESTAMENT: JOHN 10:11, ROMANS 13:1. HEBREWS 13:17.] See Scripture Appendix, page 101.

Don't Despise the Day of Small Things

God posed this question to the prophet Zechariah in the fourth Chapter, Verse 10: "Who with reason despises the day of small things?" God has Zech tell the people that Zerubabel had laid a foundation for rebuilding the House of God, and it would be his hand that would complete it. Laying the foundation was a small start to an enormous task and God had to encourage the people to *keep going*. Foundations are laid at the start, beginning or First. Everything starts as a seed. *Greatness begins as a seed.* That's why the Lord says, "He that is faithful in little shall be ruler over much." At the beginning of a thing, it's small or manageable enough for you to handle. It's also a time when you can make the mistakes that are inevitable when you step out to do something you've never done before, and from these mistakes you gain beautiful nuggets of wisdom. Finally, you are *proven* through stewardship and faithfulness over the small. Obey the Lord in the small things and watch the growth!

[**Referenced Scriptures**: OLD TESTAMENT: ISAIAH 60:22. ZECHARIAH 4:6-10. NEW TESTAMENT: LUKE 16:10-11.] See Scripture Appendix, page 102.

Chapter 2

Search Out the Resources

After you've spent that time in separation, preparation and getting things in order, it's time to get the right information, tools and training to carry out the vision.

Get Knowledge and Understanding

Some of you may find that the vision is overwhelming and God is flooding your heart with "to dos." It's prolific (ideas are coming fast and furious!) and feels like you have to run to keep up with God! Be sure to write down (or whatever your method is for recording invaluable information) what God is saying and He will give you specific instructions at specific times to carry out every phase of the ministry. He will also bring specific people and books, tapes, etc. into your life at specific times and for some of you, dreams and visions to encourage, refresh, strengthen, mobilize, build character, stretch, comfort, shape and yes even shake, etc, etc, etc! God is excited about your development and He is sure to take care of the investment He has made in you.

[Referenced Scriptures: OLD TESTAMENT: PROVERBS 8:17, 15:14, 18:15, 28:2. NEW TESTAMENT: ACTS 17:27. COLOSSIANS 1:9.] See Scripture Appendix, page 102.

Be Skillful

TAKE CLASSES ... in Team Building, Leadership, Communication, and other subjects that will improve your skills as a **leader** and teacher. For dance, if you haven't already, you should have a good, solid foundational ballet class. Then, *continue your education* through ongoing study, dance and otherwise. I take classes fairly regularly *in addition to* my rehearsals. Skill in dance is a tool that lessens the possibility of injury. In addition, as you increase your level of excellence in dance, it will give you greater breadth in terms of how God can use you. Be SKILLFUL, BE EXCELLENT!

Also, one should have a working knowledge of the human body, how it functions and how to identify sprains along with some basic knowledge on how to treat minor injuries.

[Referenced Scriptures: OLD TESTAMENT: PROVERBS 16:23. DANIEL 1:4&17, 9:21-23. NEW TESTAMENT: ROMANS 15:4] See Scripture Appendix, page 103.

Ask God for the Right Help

Whether you're teaching choreography or God's Word, have at least one anointed assistant with you while you're teaching — preferably someone you're mentoring. Having someone on hand to assist helps you keep your focus on just the teaching and simultaneously, gives you an opportunity to pour into someone else whom God has put in your life worthy of your time and the anointing on your life. Just look at Jesus and the disciples, Elijah and Elisha, Moses and Joshua! They were committed to help because they had the revelation that their destiny was tied to that ministry.

[Referenced Scriptures: OLD TESTAMENT: 1 KINGS 19:19. 2 KINGS 2:1-9. PSALM 121: 1-8. NEW TESTAMENT: MATTHEW 9:9] See Scripture Appendix, page 104.

Chapter 3

The Divine Covering
Garments in Ministry

The Holy Spirit is the Pattern Maker (more on this in the section on Choreography)! One of the most exciting studies in the Word is the study of garments and what they symbolize.

Let's start in the Word of God at the first mention of a "coat" or "covering." The first mention is in Genesis, the book of beginnings. We see in Chapter 2, verse 25 that, "They [Adam and Eve] were both naked, the man and his wife, and were not ashamed." They were naked, yet they were not ashamed because in actuality they were "covered" or "clothed" in *innocence or sense of right standing with God - this is also that "Robe of Righteousness".* They didn't have a "sin consciousness," which causes the filthy stain of sin to linger in our minds long after we ask for forgiveness. They had no knowledge of evil or sin so there could be no shame. However, in Chapter 3, *after* they sin, the Bible says their eyes were opened. They came out from under the covering of innocence and knew they were naked. Ashamed, they sewed fig leaves together and made themselves aprons or loin clothes. In an attempt to cover their nakedness — or really, their *sin* — they patched together those fig leaves (which are pretty large leaves!) to cover their loins. That was fairly clever, but it wasn't going to do the job. Today, we refer to the "fig leaf" when something is said to be insufficient for concealment or camouflage.

We have to cover up the way God has prescribed in order to be covered properly. God stepped in and gave Adam and Eve proper coverings in Genesis 3:21, where the Bible says that God Himself made "coats of skins" and He clothed them. Innocent animal flesh had to die, and blood had to be shed in order to "cover" Adam and Eve's sin. Only God can re-cover us (or cover us up again) when we've gotten separated from Him and only He can return us to being separated <u>unto</u> Him.

As you continue to read, I pray that the Lord reveal to your spirit how very important the garments are to us as dance ministers. There is a reason the scripture speaks of the garment of praise for the spirit of heaviness. There is a reason God was so very specific with the priests on not just the pattern of their garments but the fabric that was to be used as well. There are specific principles and guidelines that are in the scripture that we can follow concerning our garments that please God. The reality is that unless we follow God's pattern or *prescription*, we will not have the cure. The scriptures also talk about the sicknesses that could be in the garments and in the New Testament, healing virtue was in fabric that was prayed over. Stick with the Lord and me -- this will be explained more later on. Let us now take a little journey through the bible on prophetic garments.

[**Referenced Scriptures**: OLD TESTAMENT: GENESIS 2:25, 3:21, ISAIAH 61:10.]
See Scripture Appendix, page 106.

Our Garments Should Speak!

In a Dance Ministry, the garment worn must also minister; it should agree with the song, movements, etc. It should be *prophetic*.

Joseph's Coat Spoke!

Joseph was so excited about his father's gift of a new coat! It was a wide coat that reached to the palms of his hands and the soles of his feet. He probably dragged that coat around with him everywhere and most likely looked pretty silly in it! Now why did his father give him such a big coat? *(Remember my definition of prophetic:* "God Speaking," both to our right-now and our future or destiny.) Joseph's was a coat of many colours, which meant "many breadths." In other words, the coat was very wide. It was like a flag that shows the colors of one's nation. It was emblematic and it symbolized ruler-ship and dignity. The Hebrew word for colours is *pac* and it is the same word that is used to describe the coat Tamar wore in 2 Samuel 13: 18-19. Tamor was the king's daughter and this is what the king's daughter would wear because of her royal station.

At the time the Bible was written, it was customary for the father to name the child (as mentioned previously) and that the name would be prophetic. The father would also speak a prophetic blessing over his children at the end of his life. Well, *Joseph's father went a step further* and put Joseph's destiny on his back (literally) long before the boy could live up to it or even fit into it! Isn't that what God does for us? Destinies or callings are revealed to us that we couldn't dare think possible; yet God would have us "wear [our destiny] spiritually" *now,* because He wants us to "grow into it" and trust Him to realize it through us.

We know that Joseph went through a season of preparation for ruler-ship. Read Genesis 37 to find out what Joseph went through — can someone say *"pro--cess"?!* Think of a food processor, how it breaks down the stuff that is hard to digest ... yes, *now* you've got the picture. If God is preparing you to rule — and He is — get ready to spend some time being envied, misunderstood, harassed, cursed out, forgotten, overlooked, left out, etc. God will surely use it to break down and get rid of the stuff that He doesn't need.

God would speak to Joseph as a boy through dreams and gave him a dream that spoke of him ruling. Before he grew up spiritually (or matured), Joseph shared this dream of ruler-ship with his brothers who already resented and hated him because their father favored him, he was the only one that received the "Coat Blessing". *Be watchful of the haters when God is raising you up, and be very prayerful and careful with whom you share your dreams and visions. Also, while we're on the subject of being cautious, be very careful where you agree to minister. Check it out in prayer and physically - ahead of time.*

Back to Little Joe, Instead of revealing his dream before the time, Joseph should have pondered that dream in his heart (like Mary did when the Angel of the Lord visited her and told her what was going to happen…Mary was a young girl but she had wisdom beyond her years).

In Genesis, Chapter 37, verse 23, poor Joe is stripped of his coat and thrown in a pit. The haters, *his own brothers,* put blood on the coat and took it back to their father. That coat was symbolic of Joseph's destiny, so the devil was trying to say he wouldn't rule. When dad saw the coat he said, "This is my son's coat." It was the identifier! God was, however, working it out all along.

In Chapter 39, we see more "processing" of little Joe when he encounters Potipher's wife and had to leave his garment behind (again!) — The devil is a liar! He had to leave his garment in hot mama's hands to get away from her. Here again, that garment was the identifier because she used it to prove that he had been there and accused him of trying to force her into lying with him (she was lying on him because he refused to "lie with her.") Joe had to go down *again* (there's a pattern here), as he gets stripped of his coat AGAIN (how many of us are willing to give up the prophetic symbol in our lives to flee sin??? I'm beginning to have much respect for Joe about now). Then he got thrown into another "pit" — this time it was *jail.*

The beautiful thing about this pattern is that God keeps getting him out, but not until little Joe gleans some nuggets of wisdom. *This* was the way in which God chose to get the wisdom to him. God is so good! In Chapter 41:37-46, after 13 years of "processing," he *finally* became ruler. In verse 42, Pharaoh gives him his ring and places on his back vestures of fine linen — that particular vesture was one that was placed on dignitaries and rulers. *He finally fit into that coat his dad gave him 13 years earlier.* Pharaoh said to Joseph, "See, I have set thee over all the land." That day, Pharaoh put a coat upon him, one that signified his rule. Joseph's prophetic dream was now manifesting — his father spoke it prophetically by throwing the coat over him as a boy.

[**Referenced Scriptures**: OLD TESTAMENT: GENESIS 37, 39, 41:37-46. 2 SAMUEL 13: 18-19. NAHUM 2:3.] See Scripture Appendix, page 107.

Samuel's Garment Spoke Too!

In case you're unfamiliar with this text, I'll give you a little background. Samuel came about as a result of his mother Hannah's cry out to God for a child. She was barren. During this time, there was hardly any thing that was more shameful than being barren. One was said to be "cursed". God was gracious and answered Hannah's heart cry and blessed her with Samuel. She in turn, gave Samuel back to the Lord and he served the Lord under Eli the priest as a very small boy. Yes, God answered her prayer but HE had big plans for this little package of joy!

Samuel was destined to be a prophet and, as such, God dealt with him very early in his life, and He dealt with him prophetically (no small wonder). As a child, Samuel began hearing the call of God as many of you did when you were children. I know I did.

Samuel's mother had the prophetic word for Samuel as she made him a little coat. The word *coat* in the Hebrew is *Me'iyl* and is described as the garment worn by men of rank or the high priests. He was a child but that coat signified him as a high priest or a man of rank! Like Joseph, though he started out as a child, he grew into that "coat" and served as a mighty prophet. If you look at Samuel a little more closely, you will find that God used him mightily even while he was still a child - he gave him a hard task too. He had to pronounce judgment on his own mentor.

As mentioned previously, everything starts as a seed. That's one reason why we can't afford to despise anyone's youth or think that God can't use children. We had better take notes and meditate on what is said when God begins to use children in ministry. He's going to use them like never before because they don't have their own agenda and He can get a pure, sure Word through them! *For those of you who are working with the little treasures, I'll talk more about children in dance ministry in one of my next books -- they have a ministry!*

[Referenced Scriptures: OLD TESTAMENT: 1 SAMUEL CHAPTERS 1, 2 & 3. See Scripture Appendix, page 112.

David's Ephod Spoke His Heart!

King David danced before the Lord in a linen ephod[†]. Just how prophetic was that? In addition to being a King, David was a man of war, a worshipper, a palmist, a minstrel (he played his instrument and evil spirits would depart), a man after God's own heart and it was his blood line through which Jesus would come, He came through the tribe of Judah. David is a wonderful character study but what is most relevant here is when my boy DANCED and what he had on WHEN he danced...that Prophetic Linen Ephod.

As mentioned earlier, when Joseph came into rule, Pharaoh put a vesture of fine linen upon him. Throughout the Scriptures, we see that the garments of priests, dignitaries and the wealthy were made of "fine linen." Since we know full well that everything God does is purposeful, there must be a specific reason for using linen as opposed to, say, wool or polyester! Linen is made from the flax plant. It is defined in Hebrew as "white linen" and, further, comes from the Hebrew word *badal*, which means "separated" or "isolated" because of its divided fibers. Oh, the fibers were divided or separated! This symbolized a life that was separated from sin and separated to the service of the Lord. I heard someone once say that linen was useful because it was porous and the air could flow through the garment freely to eliminate sweating (again, this is symbolic of God doing the work instead of us trying to make something happen or doing His Work in our strength) that, by the way, is extremely dangerous. I know because I've done it and I learned God's mercy on a whole new level! Thank God for His mercy.

So you see ... 2 Samuel 6:14 says, "And David danced before the Lord with all his might; and David was girded with a linen ephod." The symbolism here with David is a little different than the symbolism of Joseph and Samuel. Here, the linen designated the priesthood or servitude. David was bringing the Arc of the Covenant back home, this represented the presence of the Lord and a brotha was H-A-P-P-Y! Dancing in that linen

---

[†] An ephod is a linen apron worn in ancient Hebrew rites; especially a vestment for the high priest.

ephod was symbolic of David's desire to serve the Lord and lay aside his royalty to do so! The king knew full well that he needed God's presence more than his own dignity. Stripping himself of his dignity by taking off his royal robe and rejoicing before the Lord in that linen ephod was symbolic of consecration, separateness, and servitude! His garment when he danced before the Lord, SPOKE!

David's wife Michal, however, thought it was *lewd* for the King to dance like he did and in what he had on. (She was a problem!) In 2 Samuel 6:16, we see that Michal despised him for that wild dance in that ephod. She was a king's daughter and a king's wife. She was "royalty" and couldn't understand exchanging royalty for celebrating God's presence. She had no idea who David really was and what that arc truly represented...if she was around today, we would say she was "in the flesh" and clueless! *Much like those who criticize **you** for dancing with all of your might before the Lord!* Things didn't work out too well for Michal after that!

When we dance in ministry, what is on our backs should SPEAK too! Our garments should agree with what God has placed in the music, in our hands, our hearts and our feet. I have a war dance that I minister that is about the Awesomeness of God. The garment I wear is red; it looks like blood and fire. Red, not for the blood of Jesus, but red relative to the blood of the enemy; see Nahum 2:3 where it says, "The shield of thy mighty men is made red and His valiant men are in scarlet." This was a prophetic statement made by the valiant men that the enemy's blood was about to be shed. You might ask, "How does our enemy (the devil's) blood get shed?" We take him out in the spirit realm — he's a spirit and our obedience is an awesome weapon. Obeying God's way of doing things is an act of violence against the forces of darkness and it protects the anointing! My red garment speaks exactly that: our God in His awesomeness, fearsome, a man of war, the Lord of the Hosts is about to create a spiritual blood bath. In other words, "See this red devil? You are about to get taken out!" I love God — He is not playing!

[**Referenced Scriptures**: OLD TESTAMENT: 2 SAMUEL 6:14&16. See Scripture Appendix, page 118.

The Priestly Garment

God is absolute and very specific and, as mentioned, He has purpose for EVERYTHING that He does. The priesthood is outlined throughout Leviticus and there is much there regarding the garments. I'll touch on some things here that I believe are key in principle to you as a minister of dance that you and your garment minister may want to review.

> They [priests] were instructed that the weaves were not to be co-mingled. Specifically, God had said not to mix wool with linen. Again, linen represented a fabric that was divided or separated, but wool mixed with the linen made a whole different garment and was strictly forbidden.
>
> God often warned the priests to inspect the garments, as diseases (specifically leprosy) can lay resident in the garment, just as healing can. (See our study on the "hem" of the garment toward the end of this chapter.)

[Referenced Scriptures: OLD TESTAMENT: LEVITICUS 19:19. DEUTERONOMY 22:11. JOB 30:18.] See Scripture Appendix, page 118.

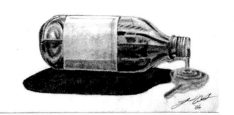

The Anointing on the Garment

To *anoint* means "to rub or smear on." The anointing is on the Word of God, and Jesus is the Word, He is also the Christ, which means Anointed One. Jesus is our modern day high priest who sent the Holy Spirit (or the "Comforter") who is the Anointing. So, I'm in the Word, studying to show myself approved unto God, a workman that need not to be ashamed rightly dividing the Word of God and I'm in His Presence, I'm rubbing shoulders with Him and He's rubbing off on me and, therefore, I'm anointed by the Anointing and the Anointed One! [Excuse me a moment, I just want to praise the Lord for Jesus and the Holy Spirit and ALL they have done for us!!! Praise you LORD]. With whom are *you* rubbing shoulders?

With each ministry piece that God gives you, you will find that the anointing, in particular, could be on the person ministering, the song or music, a particular place in the song, a particular person in the group, or on the garment in particular. By "in particular" I mean that although the anointing will certainly be on *you* and the piece in general, there are times — oh, my God, as He wills — when the anointing would fall at a certain point, with a certain movement and when the *garment* is moved in a particular way. I have a piece the Lord Jesus gave me in which I use Donald Lawrence and Tri City Singers' song, "Can I Lay in Your Arms." This has awesome choreography but it's when Jesus walks out with the dancer in His arms, that the anointing, in particular, falls and takes all of us to an unbelievable place — oh my God! A place where His presence is so evident, tangible, heavy, ahhhh, I live for that! We live for that! For this section though, I'll go back to my red garment that I use for the song about the awesomeness of God — when I put that garment on I can tangibly sense the anointing fall.

Let's look at what happened in the Scriptures when the anointing was on or in the garment, down at the bottom (or hem) of the garment, no less! The word *hem* in Greek is *Kraspedon* meaning a "margin, specifically a fringe, tassel, border or hem." In the Hebrew the word hem is *Shuwl*, it means "to hang down," implying a bottom edge, hem, skirt or train.

Psalm 133 talks about the precious ointment upon the head that ran down upon the beard (even the high priest Aaron's beard), then went down to the skirts of his garments. I must mention the woman with the issue of blood who said within herself, if she could "but touch the hem of Jesus' garment."

In the New Testament, look at what happened with the handkerchiefs and aprons in Acts 19. In Verses 11 and 12, God wrought special miracles by the hands of Paul so that from his body were brought unto the sick handkerchiefs or aprons, and the diseases departed from them, and the evil spirits went out of them. They were bringing cloths to Paul and placing them on his body. Healing virtue that God had in Paul's body was transmitted to the cloths (handkerchiefs and aprons) and when the cloths were brought to the sick people and those who had evil spirits, they were cured! The anointing to heal and cast out devils (to do miracles) was in the cloths!

The bottom line (pardon the pun!) is that the anointing *can* abide on the *garment*, but what's more important is the garment is anointed because the garment is on *you!* You ARE anointed.

Lastly, I encourage you to pray over your garments and set them apart, to dedicate them to the Lord for HIS exclusive use. He will honor your stewardship and care. (You don't want to mix the use!)

[**Referenced Scriptures**: OLD TESTAMENT: PSALM 133. NEW TESTAMENT: ACTS 19:11-12. 1JOHN 2:27.] See Scripture Appendix, page 119.

Who's Handling the Garment?

It's extremely important that you pray about who handles your garments. I have a *garment minister*. She is someone who loves the Lord first, loves us, loves the ministry of dance, and is very skillful.

This garment minister reminds me of Dorcas. In the New Testament (Acts 9;36), the Scripture refers to Dorcas, whose name means "clear sighted like a roe." Dorcas was a disciple and full of good works. When she died, the Bible says that all of the widows approached Peter weeping and showing him the garments she made for them while she was alive. Dorcas was, no doubt, very generous because the widows were poor and couldn't necessarily afford such things. This speaks clearly of her character and devotion to the things of God. Our garment minister is so very generous and selflessly gives of herself to minister to us with the garments.

Our garment minister also reminds me of Bezaleel and Aholiab. Aholiab was the one of the two who was a worker of fabrics with embroidery and in fine linen. In Exodus 31, the Lord gives Moses the pattern for the tabernacle and God called these two by name to come to bring the pattern to reality. In the first two verses of the 36th Chapter, we read, "Then wrought Bezaleel and Aholiab and every wise hearted man in whom the Lord had put wisdom and understanding to know how to work all manner of work for the service of the sanctuary, according to all that the Lord had commanded."

So pray for God to show you who your garment minister is — indeed, it could be a *team* of garment ministers. The first clue for me was that she loved the ministry and the dance ministers…and when we looked at her work, we could see the anointing. It's one thing to be a skilled garment maker but it's something else altogether when that person has God's spirit of wisdom and understanding to do the work!

You may start your ministry off by buying pre-made garments in which to minister, but eventually having your own garment minister (who is set apart for this work and sanctified in it) is as key as the garment itself and, as you now know, is critical to the ministry of dance. The wrong garment — wrong color, wrong fabric, wrong cut, etc. — could be contrary to what God is saying, but the person with the spirit of Aholiab, who is skillful, sanctified and appointed by God will flow with the Holy Spirit. Pray for someone with the spirit of Dorcas who is able to see the vision clearly and bring forth that which speaks in agreement with the ministry and is full of good works.

The garment minister should also be well compensated for his or her ministry and craft. In Exodus 36:3, the Scripture says that the "people brought such a huge offering for the work of the sanctuary that Moses had to make a proclamation that no one was to bring anymore for the work." They recognized the value of the work and freely gave. Let's show appreciation and value our garment ministers! The laborer is worthy of his or her hire.

[Referenced Scriptures: OLD TESTAMENT: EXODUS 28:3, 31:1-10, 36:1-7, 38:23. NEW TESTAMENT: LUKE 10:7. ACTS 9:36.] See Scripture Appendix, page 119.

Chapter 4

Discernment is a Key —
Things to Watch For

As you move deeper into the things of God and, perfecting the ministry, you become a threat to the enemy. As such, you will need a greater level of discernment (ability to see beyond the surface). In other words, you need to be able to recognize people's motives and deal with them wisely.

The Luciferian Spirit

This is the spirit that wants to be seen and wants to upstage God. In Isaiah 14, Lucifer, whose name meant "Light Bearer," said in his heart that he would ascend into heaven and exalt his throne above the stars of God. He said, "I will ... I will ... I will ... be like the Most High." It's *pride to the third degree* when we self-exalt, and we know a haughty spirit comes before the fall because in verse 15 we see where the bible says, "he would be brought down to hell, to the sides of the pit!" No Lord, not my will but *Thy* will. Jesus must increase and I must decrease.

As dance ministers, it is VERY easy to get puffed up, full of hot air, wanting to do things by the will of flesh instead of the will of God, partially because our bodies are involved and, typically, because we as dancers are taught to "hit it" after the "5, 6, 7, 8 ... ." If you've had formal training, the objective has usually been to make it to film or stage for fame, fortune, etc. We've been trained with the proverbial "carrot" to get to Hollywood or Broadway. God wants to perform His Word through us, so we must be sure we're not performing our will in "His Name."

Notice that Lucifer kept saying, "I will...I will." He said not *Thy* will but *my* (or his) will, Lord. That's why he had to go down.

[**Referenced Scriptures**: OLD TESTAMENT: PROVERBS 16:18. ISAIAH 14:11-15. EZEKIEL 28. NEW TESTAMENT: JOHN 3:30.] See Scripture Appendix, page 121.

Witchcraft

As I've said, we as dance ministers are an extremely effective visual tool for communicating the Word of God to people who are deaf to or can no longer hear the preacher because of sin or oppression from the forces of darkness. The "deaf" are able to get God's Word from the "visual" Word moving before them through dance and drama (drama is also extremely effective - we combine both arts).

Because this is such an effective way for people to get free and ministered to, the enemy is looking for whatever way he can to stop the ministry. And we need to know that witchcraft is alive and well in the local church, in particular. Yes, there are people who **knowingly** serve satan to speak curses against God's people. We had, therefore, better be aware and know how to pray against it. This is why it's so important for us to be and have intercessors - people who know how to pray with authority and biblical knowledge. It's also important to have proper covering (a prayer covering, properly covered with the right garments and covered by your overseer).

You have a vicious enemy who is not out to merely stop you but to take you and anyone connected to you out!!! There are also people who worship Satan and are sent on assignment to take you out. Oh, and it's in the church as well, there are those who are used by the enemy in what's called "charismatic witchcraft." This is a spirit of control that can manifest through the Christian without them really knowing what's going on.

I'm sharing this with you, not so that you would be afraid, but because the GREATER ONE lives inside of you. We are not to fear the enemy, but to be aware, discerning and prayerful against him. We rule, and whatever <u>we</u> bind on earth is bound in heaven. We have delegated authority on the earth to bind and loose! To bind means to stop or hold back, to loose means to release.

Lastly, the greatest defense against the attack of the enemy is to make sure your "love walk" is intact. Walking in love, forgiving, having mercy on people is a key to keeping your heart clean. Also, build yourself up on your most Holy faith by praying in the Holy Ghost according to Jude 1:20. We must be built up for the fight! Being filled with the Holy Spirit with the evidence of speaking in other tongues is highly advisable. See the Appendix at the end with a study you can do for yourself on the Holy Spirit and the wonderful prayer language that is uniquely yours to talk to your Heavenly Father and pray His Perfect Will. *Don't miss out on this precious and powerful benefit of being born again plus it will give you POWER and DISCERNMENT in ministry.*

[Referenced Scriptures: NEW TESTAMENT: MATTHEW 10:28, 12:29, 18:18. JUDE 1:20.] See Scripture Appendix, page 123.

Competitiveness and Covetousness

These are common dangers! Again, by virtue of our creativity, we sometimes desire to achieve more and more, and in so doing, there are times when we want to out-do one another. It's become evident what that can lead to ... FLESH ... and in our flesh dwelleth no good thing, as it is enmity against God and He would be no where in that! Stay on your face before the Lord and He'll give you what you need to always keep on top of things. He will give you the "cutting edge" and you will be able to celebrate the successes of others instead of trying to out-dance them or longing for what they have.

Comparisons

Please don't compare dancers! Each person is uniquely qualified to be on the team and each brings his or her own special graces that should be encouraged! Each also has weaknesses that should not be magnified but *strengthened.*

Envy, Jealousy and Strife

Envy, jealously and strife are all very deadly offenses that can open a door for the enemy to bring sickness and disease. They can eat away at you like disease. These offenses are so very dangerous for each of us, and in the flesh, we are all subject to them.

As a dance ministry leader, if you haven't enforced the rules and guidelines of the ministry, your team will be out of order. If you haven't submitted to the covering that God has placed over your life, your team will be out of order. A dance ministry that is out of order can breed these sins and it can have the effect of a termite infestation! If you haven't followed the rules and guidelines yourself, your team will be out of order and you can bet on strife, envy, jealousy - so come against it and set things in order and, oh yeah, one more thing ...

The Great Rebellion!

The bottom line with Lucifer was that he was rebellious! That was the root of his evil — he didn't want to do what God called him to do; he did what *he* wanted to do. That was the problem and it produced all of the rebellious acts that followed.

When we rebel, it's because we refuse to do what God has commanded. Instead, we do OUR thing. Oh! ... Back to the will of the flesh. God is no where in it! Disobedience comes out of a rebellious heart. We've got to constantly check the condition of our hearts. Is there any murmuring going on? We don't have the answer to that — let's look to the Lord to tell us and, believe me, *He will.*

[**Referenced Scriptures**: OLD TESTAMENT: NUMBERS 16 (WHOLE CHAPTER). 1 SAMUEL 15:22-23. NEHEMIAH 9:16-17. PSALM 14:1. PSALM 51 ... PSALM 51 ... PSALM 51 (WE NEED THIS OVER AND OVER!). JEREMIAH 17:10. **NEW TESTAMENT:** JOHN 1:13. ROMANS 7:18. GALATIANS 5:19-21.] See Scripture Appendix, page 124.

Chapter 5

Are You Ready to Dance?!

What! You mean you're still with me? You're still reading??? You didn't get dis-<u>tracked</u>??? Well alright with your bad self! Praise the Lord because you made it to the Dance section. Let's face it, we love to Dance! I am so grateful that I get to show God my love by doing what I love and...HE LOVES IT! Life is good man. *Let's Dance!*

Set Rehearsal Times and Guidelines

Your rehearsals should be a time of worship and refreshing! You should expect the Holy Spirit to come in and direct your rehearsal times. They should be consistent and timely. Everyone should treat that rehearsal as though they were meeting Jesus Himself, because that's what you're doing! When we respect God and His time, He respects us and blesses us with Himself!

There should be a set of dance ministry guidelines so it is clear what is expected of each member of the team. Your guidelines should be clearly written so everyone will know what's expected, but they shouldn't be so stringent that they can't be followed. There should be grace and flexibility built into them.

The guidelines should incorporate all of the rules laid down by your under-shepherd, as well as specific guidelines for the dance ministers. Guidelines should include: living a Holy lifestyle; respecting leadership and one another; tithing (a basic requirement for all *helps ministers, which are* those who help in their respective churches as a volunteer); how garments are purchased and handled and supporting the church prayerfully. Additionally, each minister must be a worshipper and should be prepared to serve as "armor bearer" in the dance ministry for a short time like 90 days, before ministering before the Lord and His people.

If you're starting from scratch, the Holy Spirit will show you exactly what to do.

You might consider giving detailed instructions for establishing rehearsal times (check w/ everyone for times when they are and are not available, draft a schedule, identify a location, etc.—all the meeting planning details) and drafting a set of guidelines.

Don't Limit God!

I don't make the mistake of limiting what forms of dance God could use to relay a story or articulate His message. One author and scholar argues that God can only use certain types of music and instruments based on how the Tabernacle of David was established. However, we have a new covenant established upon better promises and we had better understand that God IS!

He is sovereign and can use whatever He wants to get His Word across. I was in a worship service once where God had the psalmist (singer of songs inspired on the spot) sing and then begin to scat! If you're unfamiliar with that term, take a look at the Glossary - you'll get a kick out of it.

My personal experience: By 1986, I had backslid away from God for four years. (I cannot believe that I had been that long separated from the lover of my soul — sin is horrible!) God got me back by His Love demonstrated in His Goodness and Severity. His Severity got my attention and His Goodness caused me to turn around! When I did, I had to deal with the guilt of turning away from Him in the first place, and I must admit that I didn't handle that properly. It was so hard to forgive myself. Consequently, I was overly hard on myself when I made a mistake. I remember once doing something that I thought must have really disappointed God, and He used a *secular* song to speak to my heart — it was Billy Joel's "I Love You Just the Way You Are." He was saying, "Don't go changing to try to please me. Don't try to be perfect. You'll make mistakes along the way, and as you submit your weaknesses to me, I'll perfect you and you'll be changed from glory to glory." It ministered to me so deeply and turned around my attitude about myself so completely — it gave me my joy back! What a wonderful God we serve!

I'm so glad I hadn't been told by "religious people" that God doesn't use *secular* music. I would have missed a wonderful ministry from the Holy Spirit. Many of the secular love songs that are written could really only be from God. When someone writes lyrics like, "I'll be with you forever," we know that's just not going to happen. But God, who is forever in love with us, says He'll never leave us nor forsake us! In this we can believe!

Various Forms of Dance that God Uses

I think the most controversial form of dance that is used in the church is hip hop. However, if God said to do it and you are properly covered (refer back to Chapter 3 on *Garments in Ministry*), you obey God! A wonderful and visible example of employing hip hop in worship is Chosen Generation, who minister in dance with Karen Wheaton.

For all of our technicians out there, I have a little message for you from the Lord: GOD IS AFTER YOU! He wants that skill, technique and excellence, and HE WANTS IT NOW!! God can and does use the following (and other) types of dance:

African/Cultural * Ballet * Gestures
Hip Hop * Jazz * Mime
Modern * Step * Tap

I expect that those of you who are "tapping for Jesus" to realize that it is a form of rejoicing *and warfare.* There is a sound in the spirit realm that is heard by the enemy when you tap, stomp and step on him. I'll share more about the authority of the feet in one my next books!

The Choreography

The Choreographer is the Holy Spirit. I can end this exhortation right there with the "period!" He is the ultimate arranger, designer and pattern maker as mentioned in Chapter 3. He graciously allows us to be co-creator with Him!

Choreography should be according to the Scriptures. Therefore, whatever piece you minister, you should have God's Word on it and be studied in that word. As a minister of dance, you *must* be well studied *generally* in the Word of God. In particular, you should be well studied in the Word as it relates to your piece. You should be able to articulate it to other ministers or to a full congregation prior to the ministry. Sharing from the Word prior to dance ministry sets the tone, but know too that there will be times when God will just want the *dance* to preach.

Your Choreography doesn't have to be to singing. We have choreography set to our pastor's messages, to instrumental music with the spoken word, to scripture read, to silence...that's the selah!

Choreography is given to you from the Lord and He expects you to be a good steward of it. As such, be sure you make it clear that it is not to be duplicated without your permission.

Sometimes we as Christians think it's "okay" to take something that God has given to another — in this case, choreography — and use it without his or her permission. The proper protocol, however, is to *ask permission* first, and if permission is given, be sure to *give God the Glory!* Also, acknowledge the choreographer — *that's* gracious, that's *God*.

Prophetic Choreography

Prophetic Choreography is when the choreography is speaking. All ministry choreography should speak. Whether it's God speaking through the ministry or He has spoken to us the prayer of the congregation. In other words, the dance can be a prophetic word where God is speaking through the ministry to the congregation directly or the dance is a prayer, it is speaking to God on behalf of the people (that's operating in your priesthood by the way). No matter which one, it should all have God's seal of approval or anointing on it. However, in much of the choreography God gives me to minister, He has me leave a part in it that is not choreographed. It may be a section, it could be 4 counts of 8, it could be at the end of the piece or the beginning. But it is for Him, to put in it whatever He wants. We just yield during that section and allow Him to unction us where and how to move. There are times when we can actually sense Him moving us, lifting our hand. There are times when He "gets in our feet" and we have no more control. He typically does that with a seasoned minister but He's doing a quick work in those who are bold and ready to trust Him.

With soloists, God can take the whole song or most of the song and change it up at any given time. He will give you a framework to stay within, for example, He may unction you to yield for a section of the song but only stay in a certain place on the platform or on the floor or in an aisle. He may have you give a particular person eye-contact, He loves to look at people through our eyes. He may have you simply touch someone as you move past them. When you're flowing in prophetic dance like this, don't be surprised when people look away. They "get" that God Himself is looking at them and they sometime can't bear it. Others will look away because it's so intimate and they are unable to "go there" with you. However, some will look away in disapproval...embrace that too, it's part of the cross we bear. There are others who will just weep (men will weep, children will weep). There are times when the Lord will use you to change a suicidal plan, to cause a man to go back home to his wife and children, to cause a man to change his mind from murder. I've had a person tell me that she answered the call of God on her life as I ministered. I've had people say a number of things they experience during ministry...God gets all the Glory. Some people will come and give testimony of what Great things God has done through your yielding but most, you will only know about when you get to heaven. Be careful and mindful always to give God His Glory for what He's done through you and to encourage them, especially other ministers, of how God wants to use them as well.

Flowing with the Psalmists and Musicians/Minstrels

There are times in the Worship service that the prophetic anointing falls on the psalmists and/or musicians and they begin to prophesy with the instruments. The prophetic dance falls on the dance minister, they began to move as an interpretation or their expression of what God is saying as either a response or expression of worship. This is something that God will do by His Spirit, you can't plan it. You can however, prepare for Him to use you by just yielding during your own personal worship time at home. Put on the music that touches your heart and just worship the Lord. Start with the lifting of the hands or the "Yadah". As you lift your heart and your hands, He will receive your worship and join in with you by inspiring the movement...it's the most glorious thing and just about as close to heaven as we can get on this side!!!

It's Sacred what We Do

It's sacred what we do, whatever the cost to stay on task, keeping yourself holy, keeping your heart clean, protecting the anointing, do it. Do it, do it in the ability that God gives as many lives will be changed and many lives will be saved. I often prayed that the "visual" of what God is saying will stay in the hearts of people and God will bring that "visual" back to their minds just when they need it. The dance is God's Word made three-dimensional, it's a moving picture of what He is saying. A picture is worth a thousand words but when it's a Divine Picture from our Great and Eternal God, it is impossible to put value on it. The world knows the value of the visual. Marketing strategies are based on how God designed us to take in information. Of all the senses, it's the sense of "sight" that is most susceptible to a "message". The devil has a message and he's using all of the "visuals" to deliver that message because of its effectiveness. Dance ministers are the "feet" of the Arts Ministry but most importantly, we are the "visuals". The Dance Ministry is truly an end time weapon from the Lord. It has the visual, the music, the song - all those arts involving all those senses at one time - powerful! Be good stewards over this wonderful gift -- it is a trust from the Lord.

[**Referenced Scriptures**: OLD TESTAMENT: ISAIAH 52:7. NEW TESTAMENT: ROMANS 10:15, 13:7. 1 CORINTHIANS 15:3-4.] See Scripture Appendix, page 126.

Let's Pray

Dear Father God, in Jesus' Name, I thank You for the privilege and honor to serve You in this powerful, visual ministry. I thank You for Your equipping, timing and excellence in ministry. I thank You that people are delivered, healed, refreshed, strengthened, awakened, provoked, lifted up, comforted and restored. I thank You that depression, disease, sickness, and oppression must go when I minister in the dance before You and Your people. I thank You that You will be glorified and honored, and as You give the ministry to us, we'll give it right back to You for instruction and direction, for nurturing and proper care. I thank You that all things will be worked out after the counsel of Your Own Will according to Ephesians 1:11. AMEN.

Chapter

6

Exercises and Basic Dance

There is one principle that we will look at that will position you to get the most out of exercises using the five basic ballet positions. It is this: *Use your WHOLE body to move one little toe.*

You might ask, "How do I involve my neck (for example) in pointing my toe?" Think about it, try it, and you will see that getting the whole body involved in moving just one part is *so powerful*. (Does that sound like the Body of Christ being on one accord for power and effectiveness?) Muster the strength from the neck, through the shoulders, arms, back, tush, thigh, calf and foot — all into moving that one toe! Suddenly, the toe has more power than you ever thought possible! The key is that *all of the muscles* are engaged; *that's* where the strength and control comes from.

All movement starts from the inside. The work starts internally, and the beauty, strength and power show externally.

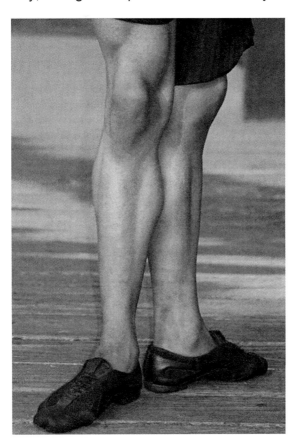

When working the arms, use all of those wonderful back muscles — when's the last time they did some work? We are so wasteful with our power! Begin the exploration of all of the muscles that are in your back. Begin to squeeze your back muscles IN ORDER TO MOVE your arm.

God has perfectly created our bodies, it is an amazing machine. You will discover more and more just how much power this amazing machine actually has!

Use your arms, back, stomach, tush and thighs for extending the leg or foot engaging every muscle in the work.

Battement Degage

And now, let's look at the fundamentals of dance ...

Breathing

One important thing about breathing: remember to do so! Fill your lungs as you are exercising and moving, especially during your dance ministry.

Proper Alignment and Posture

Pelvis forward, breast bone and navel must come together, shoulders down, head forward and you must be pulled up out of yourself — for example, if you were to slump down into the position of very bad posture and then rise up out of the slump using your center (stomach, tush and lower back), you would be pulled up.

Second Position

The oxygen flows so much better when you are upright. Oh oh, I'm preaching again! Breathe through us Lord of our uprightness!!

Stretching

Plie Demi

The very first thing you must do as a dancer is to stretch properly to prepare your body for the work. Doesn't God always stretch us before He takes us to the next level? Doesn't a woman's belly stretch before she gives birth? Don't you love the Lord for all of these beautiful analogies?!!!

Plie Grande in  **Second Position**

Five Basic Ballet Positions

Ballet is foundational for all Dance as it both engages all of the muscles and disciplines the mind. The five basic ballet positions follow with illustrations and explanations:

First Position
Feet: Back of heels touching, feet in turn-out (toes facing outward).
Arms: Extended out front, rounded just below the chest, shoulders down, hands relaxed, thumbs relaxed and nestled under fingers.

Demonstrating Feet Only

Second Position
Feet: Back of heels facing with feet apart and in turn-out.
Arms: Extended to sides, rounded just below the chest, hands relaxed, thumbs relaxed and nestled under fingers.

Demonstrating Feet Only

Third Position
Feet: Heel of one foot pulled into to instep - feet in turn-out
Arms: Same as Second, one arm is pulled in as in First position.

Demonstrating Feet Only

Fourth Position
Feet: From third position, slide front foot forward

Demonstrating Feet Only

Arms: From Third position, using the arm that was pulled in and take it up just far enough so you can look up and still see your hand.

Fifth Position
Feet: From the Fourth position, slide the foot that was moved forward back toward other foot but stop when the heel reaches the toes of the other foot, feet still in turn-out.

Demonstrating Feet Only

High Fifth
Arms: From Fourth position, lift the other arm up so that both arms are equal, again you should be able to look up and see your hands. Of course, shoulders down, arms rounded, hands relaxed, thumbs relaxed and nestled under fingers.

Feet in Releve from Fourth Position

Low Fifth
Arms: From Fourth position, bring the other arm in and lower both arms to just below and in front of the thighs, arms rounded, hands relaxed.

Some Basic Ballet Terms and Demonstrations

Arabesque. While standing on either a straight or demi plie leg, the other leg is extended behind at a right angle.

Arabesque

Ps 10:12
Arise, O LORD; O God, **lift** up thine **hand**: forget not the humble.

Attitude. While standing on one leg, the other leg is lifted to the rear, front or side and bent at a 90 degree angle.

Attitude

1Ch 23:30
And to **stand** every morning to thank and **praise** the LORD, and likewise at even;

Back Bend

Ps 9:1
I will **praise** thee, O LORD, with my whole heart; I will shew forth all thy marvellous **works**.

Battement. *To Beat:* Any extension and return of the leg.

Battement Degage

Battement, Grande

Ps 83:18
That men may know that **thou**, whose name **alone** is JEHOVAH, art the most high over all the earth.

Jete. A leap from one leg to another, both legs extended while in the air.

Psalm 18:29
For by thee I have run through a troop; and by my God have I **leaped** over a wall.

Song of Solomon 2:8
The voice of my beloved! behold, he cometh **leaping** upon the mountains, skipping upon the hills.

Lunge. One knee bent, foot usually in turn out, the other leg straight. Done is a variety of ways.

Isa 45:23
    I have sworn by myself (says God), the word is gone out of my mouth in righteousness, and shall not return, That unto me every **knee** shall **bow**, every tongue shall swear.

Php 2:10
    That at the name of Jesus every **knee** should **bow**, of things in heaven, and things in earth, and things under the earth;

Plie. *To bend* (demi and grande): A bending of the knee that is accomplished through the opening of the thighs.

Plie Grande

Ps 146:8
The LORD openeth the eyes of the blind: the LORD raiseth them that are **bowed** down: the LORD loveth the righteous:

Penche. A lean downward from Arabesque, as an example.

Ps 139:14
I will **praise** thee; for I am fearfully and wonderfully made: marvellous are thy **works**; and that my soul knoweth right well.

Releve. *To Raise:* A lifting through the foot pressing onto the ball and raising the heel.

<u>**Hab 3:19**</u>
The LORD God is my strength, and he will make my **feet** like **hinds' feet**, and he will make me to walk upon mine high places...

Reverance. A bow of any sort...However, we do so before the Lord God Almighty.

Ps 42:1
    As the hart **panteth** after the **water** brooks,
    so **panteth** my soul after thee, O God.

Ps 95:6
O come, let us worship and **bow down**: let us kneel before the LORD our maker.

Ps 96:9
O **worship** the LORD in the beauty of **holiness**: fear before him, all the earth.

Tendu. *To Stretch:* Moving the foot outward on the floor, keeping the heel on the floor as long as possible for a wonderful stretch of the foot.

Ps 94:18
When I said, My **foot** slippeth; thy **mercy**, O LORD, held me up.

Turns
Pirouette. A complete turn with supporting foot in releve or pointe, working leg has bent knee in either to the front or side.

Ps 13:5
But I have trusted in thy mercy; my heart shall **rejoice** in thy salvation.

Ps 80:19
Turn us again, O **LORD** God of hosts, cause thy face **to** shine; and we shall be saved.

Attitude

Isa 40:31
> But they that wait upon the LORD shall renew their strength; they shall mount up with **wings** as eagles

Resource: A wonderful online resource for definitions and explanations of ballet terms is American Ballet Theatre's Library at abt.org/education/dictionary/index.html. They have both still photos and videos.

Basic Laws that Govern Dance (just a sampling)

The wonderful thing about Dance is that it's based on principles or laws of truth! As you study the science or art of dance, you will find many nuggets and jewels that help in your life as a believer in the Body of Christ.

1. Law of Opposition

The Law of Opposition is used in the stretch and is a key to getting the absolute most out of our every extension. If you were to sit in a chair and stretch out your right leg, you would feel somewhat of a stretch in that leg. However, if you were to stretch out your right leg and simultaneously pull out of your waist upward and extend your left arm up, you would feel a much more thorough and effective stretch — just because of the opposition. Don't be afraid of opposition, that's where the growth comes from!

2. Engaging the Muscles-Inside Out

Muscles remember what they've done, so do it right and the same way each time. Never practice wrong. If you find you're doing anything incorrectly, don't continue. STOP ... and let the "stopping" signal to both your brain and body that the movement was incorrect. Then make the correction. Keep trying it over and over until you can do it correctly. Never ever practice it wrong; but more importantly, never ever *ever* give up on getting it done right!

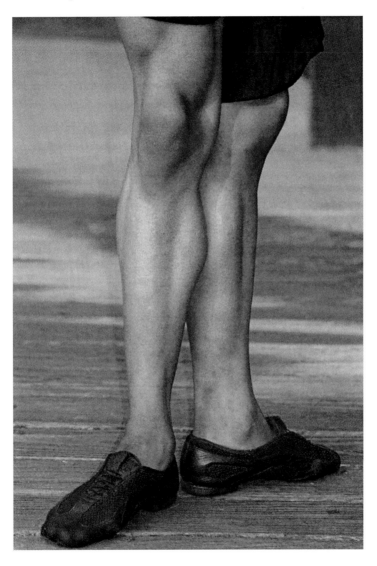

When you engage or **squeeze** the muscles, the work starts internally. Because the work is internal, it's authentic, it's true. What's then shown outward is more beautiful than ever because it started from a place of truth. When you're in a tight place, let what God put inside you, come out.

3. Downward Pressure

Downward pressure is one of the laws that govern lift in dance. Through the releve, we learn a beautiful lesson. To execute the releve, we need to press the ball of the foot into the floor, the heel automatically lifts because all of the muscles are involved in getting through the press. It's truth that we don't rise without first going down. God gives grace, gracefulness and graciousness - to the humble!

Note: I learned these principles from one of the world's greatest dance teachers, Ms. Karen McDonald of Los Angeles. We love you Karen!

Psalms 121:1-2
1 I will lift up mine eyes unto the hills, from whence cometh my help. **2** My help cometh from the LORD, which made heaven and earth.

Ps 86:10
For **thou** art great, and doest wondrous things: **thou** art God **alone**.

CONCLUSION

In Joshua 3, when the children of Israel needed to cross over the River Jordan, the Lord told Joshua to have the priests who were carrying the Ark of the Covenant pass in front of the people and lead the way. When they got up to the brink of the Jordan, the priests — the carriers of God's promised presence — were instructed to put the soles of their feet into the water and rest in the Jordan until those waters parted. Today, **we are the feet of the worshipping Arts Ministry and, absolutely, the carriers of His Glory!**

We step in the water first and stay there until God moves!

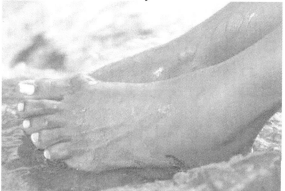

When we do, it is a frontal, offensive attack against the enemy. We will be challenged to the maximum because this is *frontline ministry*. We are doing eternal damage, so the enemy will try to STOP US! He will attempt to magnify our weaknesses before our own eyes.

God lets us know through the Apostle Paul to handle weaknesses by glorying in them. Because God's strength is perfected in our weaknesses, *we win*. The enemy will try to magnify your past failures, but God says He has new mercies for us every morning. We can "wake up" any time, including the "midnights" of our lives, no matter what the chronological time is. "Morning" is whenever there's an *awakening* in our lives. There are mercies for us there, and *we win*. The enemy will try to use the people who are the closest to us to distract and disturb us, but God is watching over the Word He's placed inside us to bring it forth in its season and *we win.* Can I be blunt? After all, we've spent some quality time together here ... so here it is: *all hell will break loose on your life* ... but the Bible says when the enemy comes in like a flood, the Spirit of the Lord will lift up a standard against him and *you still win!*

Let's talk about the standard, or banner, being lifted up over you relative to God's Grace, which is sufficient. The word *sufficient* means "to ward off or to defend through the lifting of a banner." That means He will not move the problem, but will cause us not to be moved and to stay there until we conquer the problem. You always triumph in Christ Jesus!

Another thing ... You will make mistakes. When babies are learning to walk, what do they do when they fall? They stay there forever and never get back up again and are carried around for the rest of their lives by their parents, family and friends, right? Wrong minister! They get back up! They may sit there and cry for awhile (it depends how hard they fall and what they fall on), but eventually they get back up and try it again. They may need a little help from their parents, but they try again. They may fall again and again, but they get back up again and again until, well, they win!

Proverbs 24:16 says: "For a just man falleth seven times, and riseth up again: but the wicked shall fall into mischief. "

Because of Christ's redemptive work on the cross, you are the "just" by your faith. In Hebrew, the word *falleth* is *Naphal* (pronounced naw-fal) and means: "To fall, lie, be cast down, to fail, to fall upon, attack, desert, fall away to, go away to, fall into the hand of, to fall short, fail, fall out, turn out, to settle, waste away, be offered, be inferior to, to lie, lie prostrate, to cause to fall, fell, throw down, knock out, lay prostrate, to overthrow, to make the lot fall." From any of those things, you rise just like Jesus did. He went down but He rose up, and because He takes preeminence in all things (in other words, He did everything He expects us to do, and He did it first), He rose. He rose so you must rise. *You win!* You get the picture.

Let's look at sufficiency once more, when Paul went to God three times with the thing that messed with him, that "thorn in the flesh", the Bible says that he besought the Lord and God told him "My Grace is Sufficient for you." The word "sufficient," according to Strong's Concordance means more than merely "enough" — it means that and more. It means "to ward off or avail," and it comes from the same word that means to expiate (to make amends for, do penance for, apologize for) sin. It's the idea of Grace being a barrier or standard that is lifted up against *whatever!* Can somebody say "whatever"?! That "thing", whatever it is, is blocked off by Grace. So God is saying: for this thing, Paul, don't ask me to move it, because my Grace is a barrier that stops that thing from moving you! Bless HIM! I'm preachin' myself happy! Now that's how it's done *According to the Scriptures*!

So, with this teaching, I must forewarn you and thereby, forearm you. The enemy is a formidable foe but our God is the Great and Mighty God. He knows how to navigate you around, under, over and right past the enemy in His face! In the 23rd Psalm, the Great Shepherd says He would lead us by the still waters and prepare a table before us in the presence of our enemy. Greater is He that is in you and me than he that is in the world.

[**Referenced Scriptures**: OLD TESTAMENT: JOSHUA 3-4. PSALMS 23, 149:3, 150:3-4. PROVERBS 24:16. LAMENTATIONS 3:22-23. **NEW TESTAMENT:** LUKE 12:48. ROMANS 8:27&36. 1 CORINTHIANS 2:14. 2 CORINTHIANS 12:9. 1 JOHN 4:4.]
See Scripture Appendix, page127.

One last very important thing…

I wouldn't want to take for granted that because you picked up this book you have a relationship with the Almighty Father God of All through the Lordship of Jesus Christ our Savior.

No matter who you are, *you alone* are unable to save yourself for eternity. You may be able to lock your door at night and be safe from intruders. You may be able to put so much money away each month to save up for unexpected life incidents. You may be able to do any number of things to keep you and your family safe from harm. *None* of those things, however, will ensure your eternal salvation.

God has made provision for your forever by sending His son. Jesus, who is both true God and true Man, came and poured out His Own Divine blood to purchase us out from under the servitude of Satan. We were born separated from God through the disobedience of Adam and Eve, but God planned a way of escape from a sinful nature to His Divine Nature. What a beautiful gift — *and* we get to skip hell! It's ALL good!

There is a simple prayer for one who is separated from God that is outlined in Romans 10:9-10. It requires an admission that you need a Savior that comes from your heart and is expressed through your mouth as follows: "If you believe in your heart and say with your mouth that Jesus is Lord and God raised Him from the dead, you shall be saved." It's that simple: an admission from your heart and expressed through your mouth.

Pray this prayer 'Dear God in Heaven, I believe Jesus is Lord and was raised from the dead, I accept Him as Lord of my life and thank you for it Father, in Jesus' Name.'

AMEN ... and welcome to the family! If I don't see you on this side, I'll see you in heaven!

Where the Spirit of the Lord is, there is Liberty!

About the Author

Stine McDonald is a worshipper and has been dancing prophetically since 1987 and has begun six different dance ministries for both children and adults. The ministries have been birthed from her own ministry, Steps Ordered by God Ministries and within her home church in California. Stine was called to the ministry in 1995, when she founded "Let Them Praise His Name in the Dance" and held dance ministry workshops for children. Stine has ministered to a multitude of children and their families and has seen God's hand of the miraculous working through the children. More recently, God is using Stine to stir-up and release many into ministry or into their next level of ministry with a strong prophetic anointing on her life and the mandate to ensure arts ministers recognize the value of God's Word. She hosts, teaches and trains in workshops, conferences and seminars on Dance/Arts according to the Scriptures and other areas of the Word. Stine teaches a monthly Bible Study on the Arts (all areas of the Arts) and hosts a quarterly fellowship for dance ministry leaders. Stine is building accredited curriculum for the Prophetic School of the Arts and pursuing her Masters in Divinity in Worship, Theology and the Arts at Fuller Theological Seminary in Pasadena, California.

Stine currently resides in Los Angeles and has a son, daughter-in-law, and four grandchildren. She is available for ministry both in the Word and Dance in churches, workshops, conferences, etc. Minister Stine may be contacted at Steps Ordered by God Ministries, P.O. Box 71463, Los Angeles, CA 90071, or StepsByGod@sbcglobal.net . For more information, please visit our website at http://www.stepsordered.com.

The Glossary is not intended to be a Theological Dictionary but is rather for the reader's use in bringing a greater clarity to the terms used or eluded to in this study.

Glossary of Terms
with Commentary

Armorbearer: Someone who bears (or carries) the armor of the warrior. In the days where kings went to war, they had someone to help them carry their weapons of war. It was someone who not only carried the armor but according to Easton's Bible Dictionary, they also knew how to skillfully use the armor and were known for their bravery. Today, the term is used to describe someone who is up-close and personal with a minister to help in anyway necessary. (By the way, if a person isn't a warrior, they won't require any help!). This person is typically someone whom God will supernaturally connect with the ministry, this person will have a deep respect for the ministry and minister and is greatly trusted by the minister. This person will typically travel and "bear" the armor (bags, luggage, etc.) It is a role of a trusted assistant and requires a true servant's heart. See 1 Samuel 14:1 and 2 Samuel 18:15.

Glory: The tangible, visible, manifestation of God's presence. It often manifests as smoke or a cloud and there are times during worship or a time of teaching when it appears thicker than others. The Old Testament refers to this where the Glory or the smoke was so heavy that the priests could not stand to minister. They could not stand on their feet, see 1Kings 8:11 for this account. The word Glory in the Hebrew is *Kabowd* and it means glory, honor, splendor, riches, abundance, reputation and reverence. It's rooted in the word *Kabod* which means heavy or weighty. There are times when His Glory or presence is so weighty that we can't stand. In the New Testament, the Greek word is *Doxa* and it's where we get the word Doxology. It means opinion, judgment, estimate and the corresponding praise, honor, dignity, majesty and glory. To glory also means to make one's boast in a thing.

Helps Minister: Someone who is assigned by God to help in ministry to answer any of the needs of a ministry (see 1 Corinthians 12:28). It is typically a voluntary position but can certainly be a paid position.

Ministry: Service rendered to God or Servant-hood. It is the same as the word "administration" in 1 Corinthians 12:5. It is the Greek word transliterated *Diakonia* and it means to serve like a waiter, waiting for the slightest command, with an eagerness to fulfill the request. Having a charitable heart to help others less fortunate. To fill an office of apostle, prophet, pastor, teacher, evangelist or most specifically, deacon. Another word used throughout scripture that carries the same meaning is "ministration" such as is used in 2 Corinthians 9:13 and makes reference to a liberal distribution to all.

Minstrel: Old Testament transliteration is *Nagan* and it means to strum with the fingers as one would do with a stringed instrument. New Testament transliteration is *Auletes* and it refers to a flute or wind instrument player. It is mentioned only twice in scripture by name, once in the Old Testament in 2 Kings 3:15 and in the New Testament in Matthew 9:23. Though a Psalmist can be a Minstrel also (King David was), the Minstrel differs because we see the affect the minstrel/piper caused in scripture, in addition the Minstrel refers more to the players on instruments. There was generally something that came forth after the minstrel played. In 2 Kings, the prophetic Word came forth, in Matthew 9, the minstrels were there to bring forth grief[1].

---

[1] John Gill's Exposition of Matthew 9:23 – "... this was a daughter of a ruler of the synagogue that was dead, there might be several of them. These instruments were made use of, not to remove the melancholy of surviving friends, or allay the grief of the afflicted family; but, on the contrary, to excite it: for the Jewish writers say [F1], these pipes were hollow instruments, with which they made a known sound, "to stir up lamentation and mourning": and for the same purpose, they had their mourning women, who answered to the pipe; and by their dishevelled hair, and doleful tones, moved upon the affections, and drew tears from others; and very likely are the persons, that Mark says, "wept and wailed greatly". Sometimes trumpets were made use of on these mournful occasions."

When David played skillfully on the harp for King Saul, an evil spirit departed - David was flowing in the "minstrel's anointing". In Matthew 11:17, it says "we have piped unto you and ye have not danced..." – in this case, the piping wasn't designed to bring forth grief but to bring forth the dance of rejoicing and joy!

Praise: A laudation or verbal expression of appreciation to the Lord. Laud is the root for our word "applaud". Rather than using the hands to offer an expression of approval and agreement, it's primarily verbal. However, Praise to our God is more than that, it also includes an expression that comes through the clapping or raising of the hands, through a bowing of the head, to a song sung or a musical note played. It's a tribute or a salute. It's thanksgiving in a myriad of differing forms and genres. One of the Greek transliterations for Praise is *Eulogia* – it's where we get our word "Eulogy" from and means a praise or blessing spoken over someone or something. One of the Hebrew transliterations of Praise is *Halal* and is the root of "Halleluiah". Halal means a praise of abandonment. It means to boast or to shine forth or to "act like a mad man". This pretty closely describes what David's dance with all of his might must have been like.

Some Hebrew words for Praise:

Yadah: Yad is the word for hand. Yadah means to "throw, shoot or cast" the hand. To extend the hands in thanksgiving but it is an "open hand". God loves the Yadah, it symbolizes surrender and acknowledgement that everything we get in our hands comes from Him. It also symbolizes that we are willing to release anything that He has put in our hands. Much like Abraham whom God required to give back to Him what God had given him --- his son, Isaac. Abraham didn't have to offer his son up, but he had to be willing. See Genesis 22.

Towdah: Also has to do with the hand but it is the lifting of the hand in sacrificial praise. Its root is Yadah but it can also be a hymn sung.

Tehillah: A song sung in thanksgiving and adoration. Its root is "halal" which means to shine, be boisterous, colorful, loud and beside oneself like a fool or mad man.

Barak: This is actually "Bless" and it means to kneel, bless, praise, salute. This is the bending of the knee in praise. It's interesting to note that when the knee is bent, everything goes down. The head, where the intellect, opinions, ideas, etc. abide. The heart, where the affections, desires, intentions, abide, all of this goes down with the bending of the knee, yielding it all to the Lord.

Praise Dance: What Miriam did in Exodus 14 after they crossed the Red Sea was an expression of gratitude and rejoicing in the dance. She was happy that God came through and brought them through! In the New Testament, the word that most closely describes a dance of joy is the definition of the word "rejoice". It literally means to go back and stir up your joy again. It also means to jump and spin simultaneously. For the children, I like to use the analogy of a glass of chocolate milk – the syrup is poured into a glass of milk and goes to the bottom of the glass. We are the glass, the milk is our spirit and joy is the chocolate syrup that God poured in us at the new birth. But we must many times, choose to stir that joy and I dare you to jump and spin at the same time without a smile coming on your face! The children break into laughter and giggling and it's sometimes hard to get them to stop! God wants us to laugh and enjoy this life He's given us. Go ahead, be childlike and get your joy back with a dance of Praise! There are even times when a praise dance is also a dance that moves you from sadness to gladness, start by faith and let the joy come!

In Luke 10:21, the scripture says that Jesus rejoiced in spirit. The word rejoiced is *Agalliao* in the Greek and it means to "exult or jump for joy". It's rooted in the Greek word *Agan* which means "much or greatly" and the word *Hallomai* which means to jump or figuratively to gush, leap or spring up…these are all movement or dance terms. In Luke 1:41 & 42, the bible says the babe (John the Baptist) leaped in his mother's womb when he heard Mary's greeting. The word "leaped" here is *Skirtao* and means to leap or jump for joy or to skip sympathetically as a fetus jumps in the womb. I remember being pregnant with my son who did flips in the womb. Children come here naturally dancing!

Prophet: A person - male, female, young or old, who is a mouthpiece for God. It's one of the five-fold offices discussed in Ephesians 4. It's a forth telling or declaration of what was to come, which always distinguished God's Holy prophets from the false prophets as God would confirm His Word with signs following. God also uses the prophet to expose what is happening currently or what has happened. It is always purposeful and as the Lord wills – you can't "make" God give you a prophetic word. Moses clearly functioned as a prophet as he kept delivering a word to Pharoah of what was about to happen. Plagues and death occurred as a result of not obeying God through the prophet when he was told to "let my people go". Jesus functioned as a prophet while here on earth. This is clearly shown when in John 4, he met the Samaritan woman at the well and told her that she was living with a man who wasn't her husband. He could not have naturally known this because in her own words "the Jews have no dealings with us". The bible says Miriam was a prophetess, though there is no account of her prophesying but the song of the Lord after the Red Sea miracle was a prophetic song of rejoicing and thanksgiving…God gave it to her on the spot or inspired it right there – so Miriam operated as a Psalmist (see below for definition of Psalmist).

Prophetic: The action taken or vehicle through which a prophet brings forth God's Word. That Word can be expressed through dance, drama, music, song, poetry, a sermon or literature (such as this book).

Prophetic Dance: A dance that speaks God's heart on any given matter that speaks to the people a clear Word. It can be choreographed or inspired on the spot, like Miriam when she had the song of the Lord, God also gave her the dance of the Lord. One might ask if someone needs to operate in the office of the Prophet in order to prophesy in dance, the answer is no. You can and will flow in the "prophetic" as a dance minister because God is using the arts to speak forth a clear word that people are more readily open to receive.

Psalmist: The singer or writer of songs/music from the Lord. It could be prepared or inspired on the spot. A Psalmist brings forth a prophetic song or music. The word comes from the Psalms and is the transliterated word *Mizmowr* which means melody or song. David wrote most of the Psalms in scripture along with others from the Levitical Tribe such as Asaph. David wrote many as a result of great distresses from either his own sin or the horror he faced from his enemies, particularly when he was running from his own son, Absalom, see Psalm 3:1. The trouble, sin, distresses proved him to be a man after God's own heart for even during the worst of times, he would give the sacrifice of praise.

Scatting: A form of singing in the jazz world where syllables or sounds are substituted for words and much of the time, sounds like an instrument. Mel Torme, Ella Fitzgerald and Louis Armstrong were very popular scat singers.

Under-Shepherd: A pastor or spiritual overseer. One whom God has appointed with insight for oversight in watching for the souls and caring for the sheep. Ezekiel

34 has a great deal to say about Shepherds – they are to feed the flock, tend to them, and cause the flock to lay down in peace. Psalm 23 is also considered the Shepherd's Psalm and clearly describes a Lord that watches, tends, feeds, causes a rest in green pastures and leads beside the still water. The Hebrew for this word is "Ra ah". Jesus is the Good Shepherd and they are to follow His leading in shepherding. He spoke of leaving the 99 to find the lost one. He binds up their wounds, protects from the wolves, and delivers them out of the trouble of getting caught up in fences, etc. Another thing that is spoken about a shepherd is that he/she is a friend to the flock.

War Dance: A dance that releases a decree and declaration of victory over anything. As the feet move in either a choreographed, prophetic dance or inspired prophetic movement in warfare, things are happening in the spirit realm. There is warfare in the heavenlies. It's the same principle of what happened when Joshua and his crew walked around the walls of Jericho, something was happening in the spirit realm that caused the wall to come down (see Joshua 6). Also look at how God says we take the land with our feet (see Deuteronomy 8:11).

Worship: As distinct from Praise, it is in its most basic meaning, a bowing down in homage of our Great God. One of the Greek transliterations for worship is the word *Proskuneo* and is directional as "pro" means toward. *Skuneo* in its root means "a dog" or like a dog who licks his master's feet". To crouch, to fawn. This is the word that is used in John 4 where the woman at the well encounters Jesus, he told her that worship was changing and even at that time had changed – that we worship the Father in spirit and in truth. The Father is seeking such – no longer would there be a formula of where they would go but it would come from our spirits and from a place of truth.

Worship Dance: A dance born out of a worshipper's heart. It can be any style, any tempo – not just a slow song. It can be from anyone, dancer or not, that expresses the heart of love and longing for the Lord God and whether it's done privately or publicly, from a technically trained dancer using all of their great skill or a little grandmother worshipping using just her arms while in her prayer closet, God Will receive it and it will surely Bless His heart.

Worshipper: This is a general term used for those who attend a church service for example but more specifically, it is a person who seeks after God with their whole heart. In my observation, a worshipper is someone who seeks God's hand but ultimately, they are not after his provision; a worshipper seeks God's direction or the mind of the Lord but again, ultimately, that's not what they are after. They are seeking after His Heart, His Essence, His Desires! The worshipper doesn't always ask God to bless them, they are looking for ways to bless or please God. They are seeking His Good Pleasure because they are in an intimate relationship and solely wants to do God's bidding! This is perhaps like a dog who eagerly awaits his masters return and is exultant upon his master's arrival and with great glee licks his master's feet. A worshipper will "lap like a dog" if necessary! See Judges 7:5 for a demonstration of this devotion and commitment.

Appendix A
The Holy Spirit – Be Being Filled

For those of you who haven't had the glorious experience of being Filled with the Holy Spirit with the evidence of speaking in your Heavenly language, I wanted to just give a few scriptures and share briefly on the benefits. If you're going to be effective in this warfare, you need to have all the power you can get.

Being Filled
Being "filled" with the Holy Spirit is a benefit to every believer. When we're born again, we receive God's spirit in a measure. When we ask to be "filled" with His Spirit, we become empowered by God and the evidence of it is speaking with other tongues (which is also called "praying in the spirit" or "praying in the Holy Ghost"). There are two distinctions with "tongues" in scripture. 1) It is for our personal edification and benefit and 2) for the congregation's edification. I'll just refer to the personal benefits for this particular teaching.

Being Filled with the Holy Spirit is a GOOD gift!

Luke 11:13 says "If you then, being evil, know how to give good gifts to your children, how much more will your heavenly Father give the Holy Spirit to those who ask Him?"

Here, "being evil" means that we as humans, are subject to error yet we would not give our children anything that would harm them.

This scripture tells us two things at least, the Holy Spirit is a good gift and you need to "ask".

Holy Spirit and Power
The Holy Spirit is the Power Source. Look at Acts 1:8 "Ye shall receive power after that the Holy Ghost is come upon you…"

Acts 10:38 "How God anointed Jesus of Nazareth with the Holy Ghost and with Power…"

Tongues
There is much controversy over whether speaking in tongues is for the church today. Many people who are not taught in scripture properly

speak against it or are afraid, and of course, because it's such an effective weapon in the spirit realm, the enemy fights it by attempting to spread confusion or fear. The Word of God settles all arguments.

They began to Speak
Acts 19:6 says that "the Holy Ghost came on them and they began to speak.." It was an act of their will.

Let's also look at Acts 2:4 – "and they were all filled with the Holy Ghost and began to speak…" Because it's an act of our will, we are never out of control. It's an utterance that begins to bubble up and come forth as we yield. "and they all began to speak as the Spirit gave them the utterance". The utterance is that spiritual language.

The Wonderful Benefits

We're built up like a Cell Phone Being Charged
When we're filled, we have the power source but we must be plugged in.

Jude 20 (there's only one chapter in this book) speaks of building up yourself on your most holy faith, by praying in the Holy Ghost.

When we pray in the spirit, it's like a Cell Phone plugged into the battery charger, we get CHARGED UP which means we're more sensitive to what God is saying and doing.

We Can Pray the Perfect Prayer

Romans 8:26 speaks of the Holy Spirit working together with our spirits to make intercession (a prayer for others) according to God's will – that's the perfect prayer. It also speaks to the fact that there's so much we don't know (which is the weakness) but God knows and He has the Holy Spirit pray His will through us "with groanings" or inarticulate speech. This is so exciting to me. I can pray God's will over my children who are so far away, without knowing what they need by praying with other tongues. Read Romans 8:26 and get this blessing.

So take some time to ask your Heavenly Father to fill you with His Holy Spirit, as you begin to thank Him, a spiritual language, uniquely yours, will begin to bubble up. Just yield and enjoy the journey!

Scripture Appendix - B

The Scriptures cited in this Study Guide are included here for your convenient reference. They are presented in the order in which they are referenced in the text, Introduction through Conclusion. Verses have been taken from the King James Version of the Bible (unless otherwise noted), as presented at:

http://www.biblegateway.com and http://www.bible.crosswalk.com

The Books of the Bible

<u>Old Testament</u>
Genesis
Exodus
Leviticus
Numbers
Deuteronomy
Joshua
Judges
Ruth
1 Samuel
2 Samuel
1 Kings
2 Kings
1 Chronicles
2 Chronicles
Ezra
Nehemiah
Esther
Job
Psalms
Proverbs
Ecclesiastes
Song of Solomon
Isaiah
Jeremiah
Lamentations
Ezekiel
Daniel
Hosea

Old Testament Continued
Joel
Amos
Obadiah
Jonah
Micah
Nahum
Habakkuk
Zephaniah
Haggai
Zechariah
Malachi

New Testament
Matthew
Mark
Luke
John
Acts
Romans
1 Corinthians
2 Corinthians
Galatians
Ephesians
Philippians
Colossians
1 Thessalonians
2 Thessalonians
1 Timothy
2 Timothy
Titus
Philemon
Hebrews
James
1 Peter
2 Peter
1 John
2 John
3 John
Jude
Revelation

Introduction

REFERENCED SCRIPTURES:

NUMBERS 23:19
God is not a man, that he should lie; neither the son of man, that he should repent: hath he said, and shall he not do it? or hath he spoken, and shall he not make it good?

PSALM 119:105
Thy word is a lamp unto my feet, and a light unto my path.

ISAIAH 40:8
The grass withereth, the flower fadeth: but the word of our God shall stand for ever.

ISAIAH 55:11
So shall my word be that goeth forth out of my mouth: it shall not return unto me void, but it shall accomplish that which I please, and it shall prosper in the thing whereto I sent it.

JEREMIAH 1:11-12
[11]Moreover the word of the LORD came unto me, saying, Jeremiah, what seest thou? And I said, I see a rod of an almond tree. [12]Then said the LORD unto me, Thou hast well seen: for I will hasten my word to perform it.

ZECHARIAH 7:11
But they refused to hearken, and pulled away the shoulder, and stopped their ears, that they should not hear.

MARK 13:31
Heaven and earth shall pass away: but my words shall not pass away.

JOHN 1:1
In the beginning was the Word, and the Word was with God, and the Word was God.

1 CORINTHIANS 15:3-4

³For I delivered unto you first of all that which I also received, how that Christ died for our sins according to the scriptures; ⁴And that he was buried, and that he rose again the third day according to the scriptures:

1 PETER 1:22-25
²²Seeing ye have purified your souls in obeying the truth through the Spirit unto unfeigned love of the brethren, see that ye love one another with a pure heart fervently: ²³Being born again, not of corruptible seed, but of incorruptible, by the word of God, which liveth and abideth for ever. ²⁴For all flesh is as grass, and all the glory of man as the flower of grass. The grass withereth, and the flower thereof falleth away: ²⁵But the word of the Lord endureth for ever. And this is the word which by the gospel is preached unto you.

ROMANS 10:17
So then faith cometh by hearing, and hearing by the word of God.

EPHESIANS 1:17-20
¹⁷That the God of our Lord Jesus Christ, the Father of glory, may give unto you the spirit of wisdom and revelation in the knowledge of him: ¹⁸The eyes of your understanding being enlightened; that ye may know what is the hope of his calling, and what the riches of the glory of his inheritance in the saints, ¹⁹And what is the exceeding greatness of his power to us-ward who believe, according to the working of his mighty power, ²⁰Which he wrought in Christ, when he raised him from the dead, and set him at his own right hand in the heavenly places,

COLOSSIANS 1:9-10
⁹For this cause we also, since the day we heard it, do not cease to pray for you, and to desire that ye might be filled with the knowledge of his will in all wisdom and spiritual understanding; ¹⁰That ye might walk worthy of the Lord unto all pleasing, being fruitful in every good work, and increasing in the knowledge of God;

2 TIMOTHY 3:16-17
¹⁶All scripture is given by inspiration of God, and is profitable for doctrine, for reproof, for correction, for instruction in righteousness: ¹⁷That the man of God may be perfect, thoroughly furnished unto all good works.

1 JOHN 2:20-27

[20]But ye have an unction from the Holy One, and ye know all things. [21]I have not written unto you because ye know not the truth, but because ye know it, and that no lie is of the truth. [22]Who is a liar but he that denieth that Jesus is the Christ? He is antichrist, that denieth the Father and the Son. [23]Whosoever denieth the Son, the same hath not the Father: he that acknowledgeth the Son hath the Father also. [24]Let that therefore abide in you, which ye have heard from the beginning. If that which ye have heard from the beginning shall remain in you, ye also shall continue in the Son, and in the Father. [25]And this is the promise that he hath promised us, even eternal life. [26]These things have I written unto you concerning them that seduce you. [27]But the anointing which ye have received of him abideth in you, and ye need not that any man teach you: but as the same anointing teacheth you of all things, and is truth, and is no lie, and even as it hath taught you, ye shall abide in him.

GENESIS 1:1-2

1In the beginning God created the heaven and the earth.
2And the earth was without form, and void; and darkness was upon the face of the deep. And the Spirit of God moved upon the face of the waters.

PSALM 22:3

But thou art holy, O thou that inhabitest the praises of Israel.

PSALM 46:10

Be still, and know that I am God: I will be exalted among the heathen, I will be exalted in the earth.

PSALM 119:130 (AMPLIFIED)

The entrance and unfolding of Your words give light; their unfolding gives understanding (discernment and comprehension) to the simple.

PSALM 127:1-2

[1]Except the LORD build the house, they labour in vain that build it: except the LORD keep the city, the watchman waketh but in vain. [2]It is vain for you to rise up early, to sit up late, to eat the bread of sorrows: for so he giveth his beloved sleep.

ISAIAH 48:17 (AMPLIFIED)

Thus says the Lord, your Redeemer, the Holy One of Israel: I am the Lord your God, Who teaches you to profit, Who leads you in the way that you should go.

JEREMIAH 20:9
Then I said, I will not make mention of him, nor speak any more in his name. But his word was in mine heart as a burning fire shut up in my bones, and I was weary with forbearing, and I could not stay.

EZEKIEL 37:1-10

1 The hand of the LORD was upon me, and carried me out in the spirit of the LORD, and set me down in the midst of the valley which was full of bones,
2 And caused me to pass by them round about: and, behold, there were very many in the open valley; and, lo, they were very dry.
3 And he said unto me, Son of man, can these bones live? And I answered, O Lord GOD, thou knowest.
4 Again he said unto me, Prophesy upon these bones, and say unto them, O ye dry bones, hear the word of the LORD.
5 Thus saith the Lord GOD unto these bones; Behold, I will cause breath to enter into you, and ye shall live:
6 And I will lay sinews upon you, and will bring up flesh upon you, and cover you with skin, and put breath in you, and ye shall live; and ye shall know that I am the LORD.
7 So I prophesied as I was commanded: and as I prophesied, there was a noise, and behold a shaking, and the bones came together, bone to his bone.
8 And when I beheld, lo, the sinews and the flesh came up upon them, and the skin covered them above: but there was no breath in them.
9 Then said he unto me, Prophesy unto the wind, prophesy, son of man, and say to the wind, Thus saith the Lord GOD; Come from the four winds, O breath, and breathe upon these slain, that they may live.
10 So I prophesied as he commanded me, and the breath came into them, and they lived, and stood up upon their feet, an exceeding great army.

MARK 4:14-20
[14] The sower soweth the word. [15] And these are they by the way side, where the word is sown; but when they have heard, Satan cometh immediately, and taketh away the word that was sown in their hearts.

¹⁶And these are they likewise which are sown on stony ground; who, when they have heard the word, immediately receive it with gladness; ¹⁷And have no root in themselves, and so endure but for a time: afterward, when affliction or persecution ariseth for the word's sake, immediately they are offended. ¹⁸And these are they which are sown among thorns; such as hear the word, ¹⁹And the cares of this world, and the deceitfulness of riches, and the lusts of other things entering in, choke the word, and it becometh unfruitful. ²⁰And these are they which are sown on good ground; such as hear the word, and receive it, and bring forth fruit, some thirtyfold, some sixty, and some an hundred.

JOHN 5:43
I am come in my Father's name, and ye receive me not: if another shall come in his own name, him ye will receive.

JOHN 6:63
It is the spirit that quickeneth; the flesh profiteth nothing: the words that I speak unto you, they are spirit, and they are life.

JOHN 8:28
Then said Jesus unto them, When ye have lifted up the Son of man, then shall ye know that I am he, and that I do nothing of myself; but as my Father hath taught me, I speak these things.

JOHN 10:30
I and my Father are one.

REVELATIONS 3:15-16
15I know thy works, that thou art neither cold nor hot: I would thou wert cold or hot. 16So then because thou art lukewarm, and neither cold nor hot, I will spue thee out of my mouth.

Chapter 1: Commissioned by the Lord

REFERENCED SCRIPTURES:

Consecration and Separation

PSALM 19:13
Keep back thy servant also from presumptuous sins; let them not have dominion over me: then shall I be upright, and I shall be innocent from the great transgression.

PSALM 46:10
Be still, and know that I am God: I will be exalted among the heathen, I will be exalted in the earth.

PSALM 118:23
This is the LORD'S doing; it is marvelous in our eyes.

ISAIAH 61:3
To appoint unto them that mourn in Zion, to give unto them beauty for ashes, the oil of joy for mourning, the garment of praise for the spirit of heaviness; that they might be called trees of righteousness, the planting of the LORD, that he might be glorified.

JOHN 3:30
He must increase, but I must decrease.

JOHN 6:63
It is the spirit that quickeneth; the flesh profiteth nothing: the words that I speak unto you, they are spirit, and they are life.

ROMANS 8:1-13
1There is therefore now no condemnation to them which are in Christ Jesus, who walk not after the flesh, but after the Spirit.
2For the law of the Spirit of life in Christ Jesus hath made me free from the law of sin and death.

3For what the law could not do, in that it was weak through the flesh, God sending his own Son in the likeness of sinful flesh, and for sin, condemned sin in the flesh:
4That the righteousness of the law might be fulfilled in us, who walk not after the flesh, but after the Spirit.
5For they that are after the flesh do mind the things of the flesh; but they that are after the Spirit the things of the Spirit.
6For to be carnally minded is death; but to be spiritually minded is life and peace.
7Because the carnal mind is enmity against God: for it is not subject to the law of God, neither indeed can be.
8So then they that are in the flesh cannot please God.
9But ye are not in the flesh, but in the Spirit, if so be that the Spirit of God dwell in you. Now if any man have not the Spirit of Christ, he is none of his.
10And if Christ be in you, the body is dead because of sin; but the Spirit is life because of righteousness.
11But if the Spirit of him that raised up Jesus from the dead dwell in you, he that raised up Christ from the dead shall also quicken your mortal bodies by his Spirit that dwelleth in you.
12Therefore, brethren, we are debtors, not to the flesh, to live after the flesh.
13For if ye live after the flesh, ye shall die: but if ye through the Spirit do mortify the deeds of the body, ye shall live.

HEBREWS 11:6
But without faith it is impossible to please him: for he that cometh to God must believe that he is, and that he is a rewarder of them that diligently seek him.

REVELATION 2:29
He that hath an ear, let him hear what the Spirit saith unto the churches.

Write, Read, Run with the Vision

HABAKKUK 2:2-3
2And the LORD answered me, and said, Write the vision, and make it plain upon tables, that he may run that readeth it.
3For the vision is yet for an appointed time, but at the end it shall speak, and not lie: though it tarry, wait for it; because it will surely come, it will not tarry

LUKE 1:38
And Mary said, Behold the handmaid of the Lord; be it unto me according to thy word. And the angel departed from her.

Don't Rush the Vision

HABAKKUK 2:1-3
1I will stand upon my watch, and set me upon the tower, and will watch to see what he will say unto me, and what I shall answer when I am reproved.
2And the LORD answered me, and said, Write the vision, and make it plain upon tables, that he may run that readeth it.
3For the vision is yet for an appointed time, but at the end it shall speak, and not lie: though it tarry, wait for it; because it will surely come, it will not tarry.

JAMES 2:26
For as the body without the spirit is dead, so faith without works is dead also.

The Lord Will Name Your "Baby" Ministry

GENESIS 17:5
Neither shall thy name any more be called Abram, but thy name shall be Abraham; for a father of many nations have I made thee.

GENESIS 35:18
And it came to pass, as her soul was in departing, (for she died) that she called his name Benoni: but his father called him Benjamin.

LUKE 1:57-66
57Now Elisabeth's full time came that she should be delivered; and she brought forth a son.
58And her neighbours and her cousins heard how the Lord had shewed great mercy upon her; and they rejoiced with her.
59And it came to pass, that on the eighth day they came to circumcise the child; and they called him Zacharias, after the name of his father.

60 And his mother answered and said, Not so; but he shall be called John.
61 And they said unto her, There is none of thy kindred that is called by this name.
62 And they made signs to his father, how he would have him called.
63 And he asked for a writing table, and wrote, saying, His name is John. And they marvelled all.
64 And his mouth was opened immediately, and his tongue loosed, and he spake, and praised God.
65 And fear came on all that dwelt round about them: and all these sayings were noised abroad throughout all the hill country of Judaea.
66 And all they that heard them laid them up in their hearts, saying, What manner of child shall this be! And the hand of the Lord was with him

ROMANS 10:17
So then faith cometh by hearing, and hearing by the word of God.

PHILIPPIANS 1:6
Being confident of this very thing, that he which hath begun a good work in you will perform it until the day of Jesus Christ:

HEBREWS 12:2
Looking unto Jesus the author and finisher of our faith; who for the joy that was set before him endured the cross, despising the shame, and is set down at the right hand of the throne of God.

Develop a Mission Statement

GENESIS 6:13-17
13 And God said unto Noah, The end of all flesh is come before me; for the earth is filled with violence through them; and, behold, I will destroy them with the earth.
14 Make thee an ark of gopher wood; rooms shalt thou make in the ark, and shalt pitch it within and without with pitch.

15And this is the fashion which thou shalt make it of: The length of the ark shall be three hundred cubits, the breadth of it fifty cubits, and the height of it thirty cubits.
16A window shalt thou make to the ark, and in a cubit shalt thou finish it above; and the door of the ark shalt thou set in the side thereof; with lower, second, and third stories shalt thou make it.
17And, behold, I, even I, do bring a flood of waters upon the earth, to destroy all flesh, wherein is the breath of life, from under heaven; and every thing that is in the earth shall die with violence through them; and, behold, I will destroy them with the earth.

1 Chronicles 28:11-20
11Then David gave to Solomon his son the pattern of the porch, and of the houses thereof, and of the treasuries thereof, and of the upper chambers thereof, and of the inner parlours thereof, and of the place of the mercy seat,
12And the pattern of all that he had by the spirit, of the courts of the house of the LORD, and of all the chambers round about, of the treasuries of the house of God, and of the treasuries of the dedicated things:
13Also for the courses of the priests and the Levites, and for all the work of the service of the house of the LORD, and for all the vessels of service in the house of the LORD.
14He gave of gold by weight for things of gold, for all instruments of all manner of service; silver also for all instruments of silver by weight, for all instruments of every kind of service:
15Even the weight for the candlesticks of gold, and for their lamps of gold, by weight for every candlestick, and for the lamps thereof: and for the candlesticks of silver by weight, both for the candlestick, and also for the lamps thereof, according to the use of every candlestick.
16And by weight he gave gold for the tables of shewbread, for every table; and likewise silver for the tables of silver:
17Also pure gold for the fleshhooks, and the bowls, and the cups: and for the golden basons he gave gold by weight for every bason; and likewise silver by weight for every bason of silver:

18And for the altar of incense refined gold by weight; and gold for the pattern of the chariot of the cherubims, that spread out their wings, and covered the ark of the covenant of the LORD.
19All this, said David, the LORD made me understand in writing by his hand upon me, even all the works of this pattern.
20And David said to Solomon his son, Be strong and of good courage, and do it: fear not, nor be dismayed: for the LORD God, even my God, will be with thee; he will not fail thee, nor forsake thee, until thou hast finished all the work for the service of the house of the LORD.

ZECHARIAH 4:6
Then he answered and spake unto me, saying, This is the word of the LORD unto Zerubbabel, saying, Not by might, nor by power, but by my spirit, saith the LORD of hosts

2 CORINTHIANS 4:5-7
5For we preach not ourselves, but Christ Jesus the Lord; and ourselves your servants for Jesus' sake.
6For God, who commanded the light to shine out of darkness, hath shined in our hearts, to give the light of the knowledge of the glory of God in the face of Jesus Christ.
7But we have this treasure in earthen vessels, that the excellency of the power may be of God, and not of us.

PHILIPPIANS 2:12-13 (AMPLIFIED)
12Therefore, my dear ones, as you have always obeyed [my suggestions], so now, not only [with the enthusiasm you would show] in my presence but much more because I am absent, work out (cultivate, carry out to the goal, and fully complete) your own salvation with reverence and awe and trembling (self-distrust, with serious caution, tenderness of conscience, watchfulness against temptation, timidly shrinking from whatever might offend God and discredit the name of Christ).
13 [Not in your own strength] for it is God Who is all the while effectually at work in you [energizing and creating in you the power and desire], both to will and to work for His good pleasure and satisfaction and delight.

1 THESSALONIANS 5:24 (AMPLIFIED)
Faithful is He Who is calling you [to Himself] and utterly trustworthy, and He will also do it [fulfill His call by hallowing and keeping you].

Submit the Vision to Your Under-Shepherd

PSALM 133:1-3
1Behold, how good and how pleasant it is for brethren to dwell together in unity!
2It is like the precious ointment upon the head, that ran down upon the beard, even Aaron's beard: that went down to the skirts of his garments;
3As the dew of Hermon, and as the dew that descended upon the mountains of Zion: for there the LORD commanded the blessing, even life for evermore.

ISAIAH 10:27
And it shall come to pass in that day, that his burden shall be taken away from off thy shoulder, and his yoke from off thy neck, and the yoke shall be destroyed because of the anointing.

JOHN 10:11
I am the good shepherd: the good shepherd giveth his life for the sheep

ROMANS 13:1
Let every soul be subject unto the higher powers. For there is no power but of God: the powers that be are ordained of God

HEBREWS 13:17
Obey them that have the rule over you, and submit yourselves: for they watch for your souls, as they that must give account, that they may do it with joy, and not with grief: for that is unprofitable for you.

Don't Despise the Day of Small Things

ISAIAH 60:22
A little one shall become a thousand, and a small one a strong nation: I the LORD will hasten it in his time

ZECHARIAH 4:6-10
Then he answered and spake unto me, saying, This is the word of the LORD unto Zerubbabel, saying, Not by might, nor by power, but by my spirit, saith the LORD of hosts.
7Who art thou, O great mountain? before Zerubbabel thou shalt become a plain: and he shall bring forth the headstone thereof with shoutings, crying, Grace, grace unto it.
8Moreover the word of the LORD came unto me, saying,
9The hands of Zerubbabel have laid the foundation of this house; his hands shall also finish it; and thou shalt know that the LORD of hosts hath sent me unto you.
10For who hath despised the day of small things? for they shall rejoice, and shall see the plummet in the hand of Zerubbabel with those seven; they are the eyes of the LORD, which run to and fro through the whole earth

LUKE 16:10-11
10He that is faithful in that which is least is faithful also in much: and he that is unjust in the least is unjust also in much.
11If therefore ye have not been faithful in the unrighteous mammon, who will commit to your trust the true riches?

Chapter 2:
Search Out the Resources

REFERENCED SCRIPTURES:

Get Knowledge and Understanding

PROVERBS 8:12-17
12I wisdom dwell with prudence, and find out knowledge of witty inventions.

13The fear of the LORD is to hate evil: pride, and arrogancy, and the evil way, and the froward mouth, do I hate.
14Counsel is mine, and sound wisdom: I am understanding; I have strength.
15By me kings reign, and princes decree justice.
16By me princes rule, and nobles, even all the judges of the earth.
17I love them that love me; and those that seek me early shall find me.

PROVERBS 15:14
The heart of him that hath understanding seeketh knowledge: but the mouth of fools feedeth on foolishness.

PROVERBS 18:15
The heart of the prudent getteth knowledge; and the ear of the wise seeketh knowledge.

PROVERBS 28:2
For the transgression of a land many are the princes thereof: but by a man of understanding and knowledge the state thereof shall be prolonged.

ACTS 17:27
That they should seek the Lord, if haply they might feel after him, and find him, though he be not far from every one of us:

COLOSSIANS 1:9
For this cause we also, since the day we heard it, do not cease to pray for you, and to desire that ye might be filled with the knowledge of his will in all wisdom and spiritual understanding;

Be Skillful

PROVERBS 16:23
The heart of the wise teacheth his mouth, and addeth learning to his lips.

Daniel 1:4
Children in whom was no blemish, but well favoured, and skilful in all wisdom, and cunning in knowledge, and understanding science, and such as had ability in them to stand in the king's palace, and whom they might teach the learning and the tongue of the Chaldeans.

Daniel 1:17
As for these four children, God gave them knowledge and skill in all learning and wisdom: and Daniel had understanding in all visions and dreams.

Daniel 9:21-23
21 Yea, whiles I was speaking in prayer, even the man Gabriel, whom I had seen in the vision at the beginning, being caused to fly swiftly, touched me about the time of the evening oblation.
22 And he informed me, and talked with me, and said, O Daniel, I am now come forth to give thee skill and understanding.
23 At the beginning of thy supplications the commandment came forth, and I am come to shew thee; for thou art greatly beloved: therefore understand the matter, and consider the vision.

Romans 15:4
For whatsoever things were written aforetime were written for our learning, that we through patience and comfort of the scriptures might have hope

Ask God for the Right Help

1 Kings 19:19
So he departed thence, and found Elisha the son of Shaphat, who was plowing with twelve yoke of oxen before him, and he with the twelfth: and Elijah passed by him, and cast his mantle upon him.

2 Kings 2:1-9
1 And it came to pass, when the LORD would take up Elijah into heaven by a whirlwind, that Elijah went with Elisha from Gilgal.

2 And Elijah said unto Elisha, Tarry here, I pray thee; for the LORD hath sent me to Bethel. And Elisha said unto him, As the LORD liveth, and as thy soul liveth, I will not leave thee. So they went down to Bethel.

3 And the sons of the prophets that were at Bethel came forth to Elisha, and said unto him, Knowest thou that the LORD will take away thy master from thy head to day? And he said, Yea, I know it; hold ye your peace.

4 And Elijah said unto him, Elisha, tarry here, I pray thee; for the LORD hath sent me to Jericho. And he said, As the LORD liveth, and as thy soul liveth, I will not leave thee. So they came to Jericho.

5 And the sons of the prophets that were at Jericho came to Elisha, and said unto him, Knowest thou that the LORD will take away thy master from thy head to day? And he answered, Yea, I know it; hold ye your peace.

6 And Elijah said unto him, Tarry, I pray thee, here; for the LORD hath sent me to Jordan. And he said, As the LORD liveth, and as thy soul liveth, I will not leave thee. And they two went on.

7 And fifty men of the sons of the prophets went, and stood to view afar off: and they two stood by Jordan.

8 And Elijah took his mantle, and wrapped it together, and smote the waters, and they were divided hither and thither, so that they two went over on dry ground.

9 And it came to pass, when they were gone over, that Elijah said unto Elisha, Ask what I shall do for thee, before I be taken away from thee. And Elisha said, I pray thee, let a double portion of thy spirit be upon me.

PSALM 121:1-5

1 I will lift up mine eyes unto the hills, from whence cometh my help.

2 My help cometh from the LORD, which made heaven and earth.

3 He will not suffer thy foot to be moved: he that keepeth thee will not slumber.

4 Behold, he that keepeth Israel shall neither slumber nor sleep.

5 The LORD is thy keeper: the LORD is thy shade upon thy right hand.
6 The sun shall not smite thee by day, nor the moon by night.
7 The LORD shall preserve thee from all evil: he shall preserve thy soul.
8 The LORD shall preserve thy going out and thy coming in from this time forth, and even for evermore.

MATTHEW 9:9
And as Jesus passed forth from thence, he saw a man, named Matthew, sitting at the receipt of custom: and he saith unto him, Follow me. And he arose, and followed him.

Chapter 3:
The Divine Covering - Garments in Ministry

REFERENCED SCRIPTURES:

GENESIS 2:25
And they were both naked, the man and his wife, and were not ashamed.

GENESIS 3:21
Unto Adam also and to his wife did the LORD God make coats of skins, and clothed them.

ISAIAH 61:10
I will greatly rejoice in the LORD, my soul shall be joyful in my God; for he hath clothed me with the garments of salvation, he hath covered me with the robe of righteousness, as a bridegroom decketh himself with ornaments, and as a bride adorneth herself with her jewels.

Our Garments Should Speak!

Joseph's Coat:

GENESIS 37

1 And Jacob dwelt in the land wherein his father was a stranger, in the land of Canaan.

2 These are the generations of Jacob. Joseph, being seventeen years old, was feeding the flock with his brethren; and the lad was with the sons of Bilhah, and with the sons of Zilpah, his father's wives: and Joseph brought unto his father their evil report.

3 Now Israel loved Joseph more than all his children, because he was the son of his old age: and he made him a coat of many colours.

4 And when his brethren saw that their father loved him more than all his brethren, they hated him, and could not speak peaceably unto him.

5 And Joseph dreamed a dream, and he told it his brethren: and they hated him yet the more.

6 And he said unto them, Hear, I pray you, this dream which I have dreamed:

7 For, behold, we were binding sheaves in the field, and, lo, my sheaf arose, and also stood upright; and, behold, your sheaves stood round about, and made obeisance to my sheaf.

8 And his brethren said to him, Shalt thou indeed reign over us? or shalt thou indeed have dominion over us? And they hated him yet the more for his dreams, and for his words.

9 And he dreamed yet another dream, and told it his brethren, and said, Behold, I have dreamed a dream more; and, behold, the sun and the moon and the eleven stars made obeisance to me.

10 And he told it to his father, and to his brethren: and his father rebuked him, and said unto him, What is this dream that thou hast dreamed? Shall I and thy mother and thy brethren indeed come to bow down ourselves to thee to the earth?

11 And his brethren envied him; but his father observed the saying.

12 And his brethren went to feed their father's flock in Shechem.

13 And Israel said unto Joseph, Do not thy brethren feed the flock in Shechem? come, and I will send thee unto them. And he said to him, Here am I.

14 And he said to him, Go, I pray thee, see whether it be well with thy brethren, and well with the flocks; and bring me word again. So he sent him out of the vale of Hebron, and he came to Shechem.

15 And a certain man found him, and, behold, he was wandering in the field: and the man asked him, saying, What seekest thou?

16 And he said, I seek my brethren: tell me, I pray thee, where they feed their flocks.

17 And the man said, They are departed hence; for I heard them say, Let us go to Dothan. And Joseph went after his brethren, and found them in Dothan.

18 And when they saw him afar off, even before he came near unto them, they conspired against him to slay him.

19 And they said one to another, Behold, this dreamer cometh.

20 Come now therefore, and let us slay him, and cast him into some pit, and we will say, Some evil beast hath devoured him: and we shall see what will become of his dreams.

21 And Reuben heard it, and he delivered him out of their hands; and said, Let us not kill him.

22 And Reuben said unto them, Shed no blood, but cast him into this pit that is in the wilderness, and lay no hand upon him; that he might rid him out of their hands, to deliver him to his father again.

23 And it came to pass, when Joseph was come unto his brethren, that they stript Joseph out of his coat, his coat of many colours that was on him;

24 And they took him, and cast him into a pit: and the pit was empty, there was no water in it.

25 And they sat down to eat bread: and they lifted up their eyes and looked, and, behold, a company of Ishmeelites came from Gilead with their camels bearing spicery and balm and myrrh, going to carry it down to Egypt.

26 And Judah said unto his brethren, What profit is it if we slay our brother, and conceal his blood?

27 Come, and let us sell him to the Ishmeelites, and let not our hand be upon him; for he is our brother and our flesh. And his brethren were content.

28 Then there passed by Midianites merchantmen; and they drew and lifted up Joseph out of the pit, and sold Joseph to the Ishmeelites for twenty pieces of silver: and they brought Joseph into Egypt.
29 And Reuben returned unto the pit; and, behold, Joseph was not in the pit; and he rent his clothes.
30 And he returned unto his brethren, and said, The child is not; and I, whither shall I go?
31 And they took Joseph's coat, and killed a kid of the goats, and dipped the coat in the blood;
32 And they sent the coat of many colours, and they brought it to their father; and said, This have we found: know now whether it be thy son's coat or no.
33 And he knew it, and said, It is my son's coat; an evil beast hath devoured him; Joseph is without doubt rent in pieces.
34 And Jacob rent his clothes, and put sackcloth upon his loins, and mourned for his son many days.
35 And all his sons and all his daughters rose up to comfort him; but he refused to be comforted; and he said, For I will go down into the grave unto my son mourning. Thus his father wept for him.
36 And the Midianites sold him into Egypt unto Potiphar, an officer of Pharaoh's, and captain of the guard.

GENESIS 39

And Joseph was brought down to Egypt; and Potiphar, an officer of Pharaoh, captain of the guard, an Egyptian, bought him of the hands of the Ishmeelites, which had brought him down thither.
2 And the LORD was with Joseph, and he was a prosperous man; and he was in the house of his master the Egyptian.
3 And his master saw that the LORD was with him, and that the LORD made all that he did to prosper in his hand.
4 And Joseph found grace in his sight, and he served him: and he made him overseer over his house, and all that he had he put into his hand.
5 And it came to pass from the time that he had made him overseer in his house, and over all that he had, that the LORD blessed the Egyptian's house for Joseph's sake; and the blessing

of the LORD was upon all that he had in the house, and in the field.

6And he left all that he had in Joseph's hand; and he knew not ought he had, save the bread which he did eat. And Joseph was a goodly person, and well favoured.

7And it came to pass after these things, that his master's wife cast her eyes upon Joseph; and she said, Lie with me.

8But he refused, and said unto his master's wife, Behold, my master wotteth not what is with me in the house, and he hath committed all that he hath to my hand;

9There is none greater in this house than I; neither hath he kept back any thing from me but thee, because thou art his wife: how then can I do this great wickedness, and sin against God?

10And it came to pass, as she spake to Joseph day by day, that he hearkened not unto her, to lie by her, or to be with her.

11And it came to pass about this time, that Joseph went into the house to do his business; and there was none of the men of the house there within.

12And she caught him by his garment, saying, Lie with me: and he left his garment in her hand, and fled, and got him out.

13And it came to pass, when she saw that he had left his garment in her hand, and was fled forth,

14That she called unto the men of her house, and spake unto them, saying, See, he hath brought in an Hebrew unto us to mock us; he came in unto me to lie with me, and I cried with a loud voice:

15And it came to pass, when he heard that I lifted up my voice and cried, that he left his garment with me, and fled, and got him out.

16And she laid up his garment by her, until his lord came home.

17And she spake unto him according to these words, saying, The Hebrew servant, which thou hast brought unto us, came in unto me to mock me:

18And it came to pass, as I lifted up my voice and cried, that he left his garment with me, and fled out.

19And it came to pass, when his master heard the words of his wife, which she spake unto him, saying, After this manner did thy servant to me; that his wrath was kindled.

20And Joseph's master took him, and put him into the prison, a place where the king's prisoners were bound: and he was there in the prison.
21But the LORD was with Joseph, and shewed him mercy, and gave him favour in the sight of the keeper of the prison.
22And the keeper of the prison committed to Joseph's hand all the prisoners that were in the prison; and whatsoever they did there, he was the doer of it.
23The keeper of the prison looked not to any thing that was under his hand; because the LORD was with him, and that which he did, the LORD made it to prosper.

GENESIS 41:37-46

37And the thing was good in the eyes of Pharaoh, and in the eyes of all his servants.
38And Pharaoh said unto his servants, Can we find such a one as this is, a man in whom the Spirit of God is?
39And Pharaoh said unto Joseph, Forasmuch as God hath shewed thee all this, there is none so discreet and wise as thou art:
40Thou shalt be over my house, and according unto thy word shall all my people be ruled: only in the throne will I be greater than thou.
41And Pharaoh said unto Joseph, See, I have set thee over all the land of Egypt.
42And Pharaoh took off his ring from his hand, and put it upon Joseph's hand, and arrayed him in vestures of fine linen, and put a gold chain about his neck;
43And he made him to ride in the second chariot which he had; and they cried before him, Bow the knee: and he made him ruler over all the land of Egypt.
44And Pharaoh said unto Joseph, I am Pharaoh, and without thee shall no man lift up his hand or foot in all the land of Egypt.
45And Pharaoh called Joseph's name Zaphnathpaaneah; and he gave him to wife Asenath the daughter of Potipherah priest of On. And Joseph went out over all the land of Egypt.
46And Joseph was thirty years old when he stood before Pharaoh king of Egypt. And Joseph went out from the presence of Pharaoh, and went throughout all the land of Egypt.

NAHUM 2:3
The shield of his mighty men is made red, the valiant men are in scarlet: the chariots shall be with flaming torches in the day of his preparation, and the fir trees shall be terribly shaken.

Samuel's Garment:

1 SAMUEL CHAPTER 1
1Now there was a certain man of Ramathaimzophim, of mount Ephraim, and his name was Elkanah, the son of Jeroham, the son of Elihu, the son of Tohu, the son of Zuph, an Ephrathite:
2And he had two wives; the name of the one was Hannah, and the name of the other Peninnah: and Peninnah had children, but Hannah had no children.
3And this man went up out of his city yearly to worship and to sacrifice unto the LORD of hosts in Shiloh. And the two sons of Eli, Hophni and Phinehas, the priests of the LORD, were there.
4And when the time was that Elkanah offered, he gave to Peninnah his wife, and to all her sons and her daughters, portions:
5But unto Hannah he gave a worthy portion; for he loved Hannah: but the LORD had shut up her womb.
6And her adversary also provoked her sore, for to make her fret, because the LORD had shut up her womb.
7And as he did so year by year, when she went up to the house of the LORD, so she provoked her; therefore she wept, and did not eat.
8Then said Elkanah her husband to her, Hannah, why weepest thou? and why eatest thou not? and why is thy heart grieved? am not I better to thee than ten sons?
9So Hannah rose up after they had eaten in Shiloh, and after they had drunk. Now Eli the priest sat upon a seat by a post of the temple of the LORD.
10And she was in bitterness of soul, and prayed unto the LORD, and wept sore.
11And she vowed a vow, and said, O LORD of hosts, if thou wilt indeed look on the affliction of thine handmaid, and remember me, and not forget thine handmaid, but wilt give unto thine handmaid a man child, then I will give him unto the LORD all the days of his life, and there shall no razor come upon his head.

12 And it came to pass, as she continued praying before the LORD, that Eli marked her mouth.
13 Now Hannah, she spake in her heart; only her lips moved, but her voice was not heard: therefore Eli thought she had been drunken.
14 And Eli said unto her, How long wilt thou be drunken? put away thy wine from thee.
15 And Hannah answered and said, No, my lord, I am a woman of a sorrowful spirit: I have drunk neither wine nor strong drink, but have poured out my soul before the LORD.
16 Count not thine handmaid for a daughter of Belial: for out of the abundance of my complaint and grief have I spoken hitherto.
17 Then Eli answered and said, Go in peace: and the God of Israel grant thee thy petition that thou hast asked of him.
18 And she said, Let thine handmaid find grace in thy sight. So the woman went her way, and did eat, and her countenance was no more sad.
19 And they rose up in the morning early, and worshipped before the LORD, and returned, and came to their house to Ramah: and Elkanah knew Hannah his wife; and the LORD remembered her.
20 Wherefore it came to pass, when the time was come about after Hannah had conceived, that she bare a son, and called his name Samuel, saying, Because I have asked him of the LORD.
21 And the man Elkanah, and all his house, went up to offer unto the LORD the yearly sacrifice, and his vow.
22 But Hannah went not up; for she said unto her husband, I will not go up until the child be weaned, and then I will bring him, that he may appear before the LORD, and there abide for ever.
23 And Elkanah her husband said unto her, Do what seemeth thee good; tarry until thou have weaned him; only the LORD establish his word. So the woman abode, and gave her son suck until she weaned him.
24 And when she had weaned him, she took him up with her, with three bullocks, and one ephah of flour, and a bottle of wine, and brought him unto the house of the LORD in Shiloh: and the child was young.
25 And they slew a bullock, and brought the child to Eli.

26And she said, Oh my lord, as thy soul liveth, my lord, I am the woman that stood by thee here, praying unto the LORD.

27For this child I prayed; and the LORD hath given me my petition which I asked of him:

28Therefore also I have lent him to the LORD; as long as he liveth he shall be lent to the LORD. And he worshipped the LORD there.

1 SAMUEL CHAPTER 2

1And Hannah prayed, and said, My heart rejoiceth in the LORD, mine horn is exalted in the LORD: my mouth is enlarged over mine enemies; because I rejoice in thy salvation.

2There is none holy as the LORD: for there is none beside thee: neither is there any rock like our God.

3Talk no more so exceeding proudly; let not arrogancy come out of your mouth: for the LORD is a God of knowledge, and by him actions are weighed.

4The bows of the mighty men are broken, and they that stumbled are girded with strength.

5They that were full have hired out themselves for bread; and they that were hungry ceased: so that the barren hath born seven; and she that hath many children is waxed feeble.

6The LORD killeth, and maketh alive: he bringeth down to the grave, and bringeth up.

7The LORD maketh poor, and maketh rich: he bringeth low, and lifteth up.

8He raiseth up the poor out of the dust, and lifteth up the beggar from the dunghill, to set them among princes, and to make them inherit the throne of glory: for the pillars of the earth are the LORD's, and he hath set the world upon them.

9He will keep the feet of his saints, and the wicked shall be silent in darkness; for by strength shall no man prevail.

10The adversaries of the LORD shall be broken to pieces; out of heaven shall he thunder upon them: the LORD shall judge the ends of the earth; and he shall give strength unto his king, and exalt the horn of his anointed.

11And Elkanah went to Ramah to his house. And the child did minister unto the LORD before Eli the priest.

12Now the sons of Eli were sons of Belial; they knew not the LORD.
13And the priest's custom with the people was, that, when any man offered sacrifice, the priest's servant came, while the flesh was in seething, with a fleshhook of three teeth in his hand;
14And he struck it into the pan, or kettle, or caldron, or pot; all that the fleshhook brought up the priest took for himself. So they did in Shiloh unto all the Israelites that came thither.
15Also before they burnt the fat, the priest's servant came, and said to the man that sacrificed, Give flesh to roast for the priest; for he will not have sodden flesh of thee, but raw.
16And if any man said unto him, Let them not fail to burn the fat presently, and then take as much as thy soul desireth; then he would answer him, Nay; but thou shalt give it me now: and if not, I will take it by force.
17Wherefore the sin of the young men was very great before the LORD: for men abhorred the offering of the LORD.
18But Samuel ministered before the LORD, being a child, girded with a linen ephod.
19Moreover his mother made him a little coat, and brought it to him from year to year, when she came up with her husband to offer the yearly sacrifice.
20And Eli blessed Elkanah and his wife, and said, The LORD give thee seed of this woman for the loan which is lent to the LORD. And they went unto their own home.
21And the LORD visited Hannah, so that she conceived, and bare three sons and two daughters. And the child Samuel grew before the LORD.
22Now Eli was very old, and heard all that his sons did unto all Israel; and how they lay with the women that assembled at the door of the tabernacle of the congregation.
23And he said unto them, Why do ye such things? for I hear of your evil dealings by all this people.
24Nay, my sons; for it is no good report that I hear: ye make the LORD's people to transgress.
25If one man sin against another, the judge shall judge him: but if a man sin against the LORD, who shall intreat for him?

Notwithstanding they hearkened not unto the voice of their father, because the LORD would slay them.

26And the child Samuel grew on, and was in favour both with the LORD, and also with men.

27And there came a man of God unto Eli, and said unto him, Thus saith the LORD, Did I plainly appear unto the house of thy father, when they were in Egypt in Pharaoh's house?

28And did I choose him out of all the tribes of Israel to be my priest, to offer upon mine altar, to burn incense, to wear an ephod before me? and did I give unto the house of thy father all the offerings made by fire of the children of Israel?

29Wherefore kick ye at my sacrifice and at mine offering, which I have commanded in my habitation; and honourest thy sons above me, to make yourselves fat with the chiefest of all the offerings of Israel my people?

30Wherefore the LORD God of Israel saith, I said indeed that thy house, and the house of thy father, should walk before me for ever: but now the LORD saith, Be it far from me; for them that honour me I will honour, and they that despise me shall be lightly esteemed.

31Behold, the days come, that I will cut off thine arm, and the arm of thy father's house, that there shall not be an old man in thine house.

32And thou shalt see an enemy in my habitation, in all the wealth which God shall give Israel: and there shall not be an old man in thine house for ever.

33And the man of thine, whom I shall not cut off from mine altar, shall be to consume thine eyes, and to grieve thine heart: and all the increase of thine house shall die in the flower of their age.

34And this shall be a sign unto thee, that shall come upon thy two sons, on Hophni and Phinehas; in one day they shall die both of them.

35And I will raise me up a faithful priest, that shall do according to that which is in mine heart and in my mind: and I will build him a sure house; and he shall walk before mine anointed for ever.

36And it shall come to pass, that every one that is left in thine house shall come and crouch to him for a piece of silver and a morsel of bread, and shall say, Put me, I pray thee, into one of the priests' offices, that I may eat a piece of bread.

1 SAMUEL CHAPTER 3

1And the child Samuel ministered unto the LORD before Eli. And the word of the LORD was precious in those days; there was no open vision.
2And it came to pass at that time, when Eli was laid down in his place, and his eyes began to wax dim, that he could not see;
3And ere the lamp of God went out in the temple of the LORD, where the ark of God was, and Samuel was laid down to sleep;
4That the LORD called Samuel: and he answered, Here am I.
5And he ran unto Eli, and said, Here am I; for thou calledst me. And he said, I called not; lie down again. And he went and lay down.
6And the LORD called yet again, Samuel. And Samuel arose and went to Eli, and said, Here am I; for thou didst call me. And he answered, I called not, my son; lie down again.
7Now Samuel did not yet know the LORD, neither was the word of the LORD yet revealed unto him.
8And the LORD called Samuel again the third time. And he arose and went to Eli, and said, Here am I; for thou didst call me. And Eli perceived that the LORD had called the child.
9Therefore Eli said unto Samuel, Go, lie down: and it shall be, if he call thee, that thou shalt say, Speak, LORD; for thy servant heareth. So Samuel went and lay down in his place.
10And the LORD came, and stood, and called as at other times, Samuel, Samuel. Then Samuel answered, Speak; for thy servant heareth.
11And the LORD said to Samuel, Behold, I will do a thing in Israel, at which both the ears of every one that heareth it shall tingle.
12In that day I will perform against Eli all things which I have spoken concerning his house: when I begin, I will also make an end.
13For I have told him that I will judge his house for ever for the iniquity which he knoweth; because his sons made themselves vile, and he restrained them not.

14And therefore I have sworn unto the house of Eli, that the iniquity of Eli's house shall not be purged with sacrifice nor offering for ever.

15And Samuel lay until the morning, and opened the doors of the house of the LORD. And Samuel feared to shew Eli the vision.

16Then Eli called Samuel, and said, Samuel, my son. And he answered, Here am I.

17And he said, What is the thing that the LORD hath said unto thee? I pray thee hide it not from me: God do so to thee, and more also, if thou hide any thing from me of all the things that he said unto thee.

18And Samuel told him every whit, and hid nothing from him. And he said, It is the LORD: let him do what seemeth him good.

19And Samuel grew, and the LORD was with him, and did let none of his words fall to the ground.

20And all Israel from Dan even to Beersheba knew that Samuel was established to be a prophet of the LORD.

21And the LORD appeared again in Shiloh: for the LORD revealed himself to Samuel in Shiloh by the word of the LORD

David's Ephod:

2 SAMUEL 6:14
And David danced before the LORD with all his might; and David was girded with a linen ephod.

2 SAMUEL 6:16
And as the ark of the LORD came into the city of David, Michal Saul's daughter looked through a window, and saw king David leaping and dancing before the LORD; and she despised him in her heart.

The Priestly Garment

LEVITICUS 19:19
Ye shall keep my statutes. Thou shalt not let thy cattle gender with a diverse kind: thou shalt not sow thy field with mingled seed: neither shall a garment mingled of linen and woollen come upon thee.

DEUTERONOMY 22:11
Thou shalt not wear a garment of divers sorts, as of woollen and linen together.

JOB 30:18
By the great force of my disease is my garment changed: it bindeth me about as the collar of my coat.

The Anointing on the Garment

PSALM 133
1 Behold, how good and how pleasant it is for brethren to dwell together in unity!
2 It is like the precious ointment upon the head, that ran down upon the beard, even Aaron's beard: that went down to the skirts of his garments;
3 As the dew of Hermon, and as the dew that descended upon the mountains of Zion: for there the LORD commanded the blessing, even life for evermore.

ACTS 19:11-12
11 And God wrought special miracles by the hands of Paul:
12 So that from his body were brought unto the sick handkerchiefs or aprons, and the diseases departed from them, and the evil spirits went out of them.

1 JOHN 2:27
But the anointing which ye have received of him abideth in you, and ye need not that any man teach you: but as the same anointing teacheth you of all things, and is truth, and is no lie, and even as it hath taught you, ye shall abide in him.

Who's Handling the Garment?

EXODUS 28:3
3 And thou shalt speak unto all that are wise hearted, whom I have filled with the spirit of wisdom, that they may make Aaron's garments to consecrate him, that he may minister unto me in the priest's office

Exodus 31:1-10

1 And the LORD spake unto Moses, saying,

2 See, I have called by name Bezaleel the son of Uri, the son of Hur, of the tribe of Judah:

3 And I have filled him with the spirit of God, in wisdom, and in understanding, and in knowledge, and in all manner of workmanship,

4 To devise cunning works, to work in gold, and in silver, and in brass,

5 And in cutting of stones, to set them, and in carving of timber, to work in all manner of workmanship.

6 And I, behold, I have given with him Aholiab, the son of Ahisamach, of the tribe of Dan: and in the hearts of all that are wise hearted I have put wisdom, that they may make all that I have commanded thee;

7 The tabernacle of the congregation, and the ark of the testimony, and the mercy seat that is thereupon, and all the furniture of the tabernacle,

8 And the table and his furniture, and the pure candlestick with all his furniture, and the altar of incense,

9 And the altar of burnt offering with all his furniture, and the laver and his foot,

10 And the cloths of service, and the holy garments for Aaron the priest, and the garments of his sons, to minister in the priest's office,

Exodus 36:1-7

1 Then wrought Bezaleel and Aholiab, and every wise hearted man, in whom the LORD put wisdom and understanding to know how to work all manner of work for the service of the sanctuary, according to all that the LORD had commanded.

2 And Moses called Bezaleel and Aholiab, and every wise hearted man, in whose heart the LORD had put wisdom, even every one whose heart stirred him up to come unto the work to do it:

3 And they received of Moses all the offering, which the children of Israel had brought for the work of the service of the sanctuary, to make it withal. And they brought yet unto him free offerings every morning.

4And all the wise men, that wrought all the work of the sanctuary, came every man from his work which they made;
5And they spake unto Moses, saying, The people bring much more than enough for the service of the work, which the LORD commanded to make.
6And Moses gave commandment, and they caused it to be proclaimed throughout the camp, saying, Let neither man nor woman make any more work for the offering of the sanctuary. So the people were restrained from bringing.
7For the stuff they had was sufficient for all the work to make it, and too much.

EXODUS 38:23
23And with him was Aholiab, son of Ahisamach, of the tribe of Dan, an engraver, and a cunning workman, and an embroiderer in blue, and in purple, and in scarlet, and fine linen.

ACTS 9:36
Now there was at Joppa a certain disciple named Tabitha, which by interpretation is called Dorcas: this woman was full of good works and almsdeeds which she did.

Chapter 4:
Discernment is a Key —
Things to Watch For

REFERENCED SCRIPTURES:

The Luciferian Spirit

PROVERBS 16:18
Pride goeth before destruction, and an haughty spirit before a fall.

ISAIAH 14:11-15
11Thy pomp is brought down to the grave, and the noise of thy viols: the worm is spread under thee, and the worms cover thee.

12How art thou fallen from heaven, O Lucifer, son of the morning! how art thou cut down to the ground, which didst weaken the nations!
13For thou hast said in thine heart, I will ascend into heaven, I will exalt my throne above the stars of God: I will sit also upon the mount of the congregation, in the sides of the north:
14I will ascend above the heights of the clouds; I will be like the most High.
15Yet thou shalt be brought down to hell, to the sides of the pit.

EZEKIEL 28

1The word of the LORD came again unto me, saying,
2Son of man, say unto the prince of Tyrus, Thus saith the Lord GOD; Because thine heart is lifted up, and thou hast said, I am a God, I sit in the seat of God, in the midst of the seas; yet thou art a man, and not God, though thou set thine heart as the heart of God:
3Behold, thou art wiser than Daniel; there is no secret that they can hide from thee:
4With thy wisdom and with thine understanding thou hast gotten thee riches, and hast gotten gold and silver into thy treasures:
5By thy great wisdom and by thy traffick hast thou increased thy riches, and thine heart is lifted up because of thy riches:
6Therefore thus saith the Lord GOD; Because thou hast set thine heart as the heart of God;
7Behold, therefore I will bring strangers upon thee, the terrible of the nations: and they shall draw their swords against the beauty of thy wisdom, and they shall defile thy brightness.
8They shall bring thee down to the pit, and thou shalt die the deaths of them that are slain in the midst of the seas.
9Wilt thou yet say before him that slayeth thee, I am God? but thou shalt be a man, and no God, in the hand of him that slayeth thee.
10Thou shalt die the deaths of the uncircumcised by the hand of strangers: for I have spoken it, saith the Lord GOD.
11Moreover the word of the LORD came unto me, saying,

12 Son of man, take up a lamentation upon the king of Tyrus, and say unto him, Thus saith the Lord GOD; Thou sealest up the sum, full of wisdom, and perfect in beauty.
13 Thou hast been in Eden the garden of God; every precious stone was thy covering, the sardius, topaz, and the diamond, the beryl, the onyx, and the jasper, the sapphire, the emerald, and the carbuncle, and gold: the workmanship of thy tabrets and of thy pipes was prepared in thee in the day that thou wast created.
14 Thou art the anointed cherub that covereth; and I have set thee so: thou wast upon the holy mountain of God; thou hast walked up and down in the midst of the stones of fire.
15 Thou wast perfect in thy ways from the day that thou wast created, till iniquity was found in thee.
16 By the multitude of thy merchandise they have filled the midst of thee with violence, and thou hast sinned: therefore I will cast thee as profane out of the mountain of God: and I will destroy thee, O covering cherub, from the midst of the stones of fire.
17 Thine heart was lifted up because of thy beauty, thou hast corrupted thy wisdom by reason of thy brightness: I will cast thee to the ground, I will lay thee before kings, that they may behold thee.
18 Thou hast defiled thy sanctuaries by the multitude of thine iniquities, by the iniquity of thy traffick; therefore will I bring forth a fire from the midst of thee, it shall devour thee, and I will bring thee to ashes upon the earth in the sight of all them that behold thee.
19 All they that know thee among the people shall be astonished at thee: thou shalt be a terror, and never shalt thou be any more

JOHN 3:30
He must increase, but I must decrease.

Witchcraft

MATTHEW 10:28
And fear not them which kill the body, but are not able to kill the soul: but rather fear him which is able to destroy both soul and body in hell.

MATTHEW 12:29

Or else how can one enter into a strong man's house, and spoil his goods, except he first bind the strong man? and then he will spoil his house.

MATTHEW 18:18
Verily I say unto you, Whatsoever ye shall bind on earth shall be bound in heaven: and whatsoever ye shall loose on earth shall be loosed in heaven

JUDE 1:20
But ye, beloved, building up yourselves on your most holy faith, praying in the Holy Ghost,

The Great Rebellion!

Numbers 16
Please read the whole chapter in your own bible.

1 SAMUEL 15:22-23
22And Samuel said, Hath the LORD as great delight in burnt offerings and sacrifices, as in obeying the voice of the LORD? Behold, to obey is better than sacrifice, and to hearken than the fat of rams.
23For rebellion is as the sin of witchcraft, and stubbornness is as iniquity and idolatry. Because thou hast rejected the word of the LORD, he hath also rejected thee from being king.

NEHEMIAH 9:16-17
16But they and our fathers dealt proudly, and hardened their necks, and hearkened not to thy commandments,
17And refused to obey, neither were mindful of thy wonders that thou didst among them; but hardened their necks, and in their rebellion appointed a captain to return to their bondage: but thou art a God ready to pardon, gracious and merciful, slow to anger, and of great kindness, and forsookest them not

PSALM 14:1
The fool hath said in his heart, There is no God. They are corrupt, they have done abominable works, there is none that doeth good.

Psalm 51

1 Have mercy upon me, O God, according to thy lovingkindness: according unto the multitude of thy tender mercies blot out my transgressions.
2 Wash me throughly from mine iniquity, and cleanse me from my sin.
3 For I acknowledge my transgressions: and my sin is ever before me.
4 Against thee, thee only, have I sinned, and done this evil in thy sight: that thou mightest be justified when thou speakest, and be clear when thou judgest.
5 Behold, I was shapen in iniquity; and in sin did my mother conceive me.
6 Behold, thou desirest truth in the inward parts: and in the hidden part thou shalt make me to know wisdom.
7 Purge me with hyssop, and I shall be clean: wash me, and I shall be whiter than snow.
8 Make me to hear joy and gladness; that the bones which thou hast broken may rejoice.
9 Hide thy face from my sins, and blot out all mine iniquities.
10 Create in me a clean heart, O God; and renew a right spirit within me.
11 Cast me not away from thy presence; and take not thy holy spirit from me.
12 Restore unto me the joy of thy salvation; and uphold me with thy free spirit.
13 Then will I teach transgressors thy ways; and sinners shall be converted unto thee.
14 Deliver me from bloodguiltiness, O God, thou God of my salvation: and my tongue shall sing aloud of thy righteousness.
15 O Lord, open thou my lips; and my mouth shall shew forth thy praise.
16 For thou desirest not sacrifice; else would I give it: thou delightest not in burnt offering.

17The sacrifices of God are a broken spirit: a broken and a contrite heart, O God, thou wilt not despise.
18Do good in thy good pleasure unto Zion: build thou the walls of Jerusalem.
19Then shalt thou be pleased with the sacrifices of righteousness, with burnt offering and whole burnt offering: then shall they offer bullocks upon thine altar.

JEREMIAH 17:10
I the LORD search the heart, I try the reins, even to give every man according to his ways, and according to the fruit of his doings.

JOHN 1:13
Which were born, not of blood, nor of the will of the flesh, nor of the will of man, but of God.

ROMANS 7:18
For I know that in me (that is, in my flesh,) dwelleth no good thing: for to will is present with me; but how to perform that which is good I find not.

GALATIANS 5:19-21
19Now the works of the flesh are manifest, which are these; Adultery, fornication, uncleanness, lasciviousness,
20Idolatry, witchcraft, hatred, variance, emulations, wrath, strife, seditions, heresies,
21Envyings, murders, drunkenness, revellings, and such like: of the which I tell you before, as I have also told you in time past, that they which do such things shall not inherit the kingdom of God.

Chapter 5:
Are You Ready to Dance?!

REFERENCED SCRIPTURES

Choreography

ISAIAH 52:7
How beautiful upon the mountains are the feet of him that bringeth good tidings, that publisheth peace; that bringeth good tidings of good, that publisheth salvation; that saith unto Zion, Thy God reigneth!

ROMANS 10:15
And how shall they preach, except they be sent? as it is written, How beautiful are the feet of them that preach the gospel of peace, and bring glad tidings of good things!

ROMANS 13:7
7Render therefore to all their dues: tribute to whom tribute is due; custom to whom custom; fear to whom fear; honour to whom honour.

1 CORINTHIANS 15:3-4
3For I delivered unto you first of all that which I also received, how that Christ died for our sins according to the scriptures; 4And that he was buried, and that he rose again the third day according to the scriptures:

Chapter 6: Exercises and Basic Dance

NO REFERENCED SCRIPTURES

Conclusion

REFERENCED SCRIPTURES:

JOSHUA 3-4
1And Joshua rose early in the morning; and they removed from Shittim, and came to Jordan, he and all the children of Israel, and lodged there before they passed over.

2And it came to pass after three days, that the officers went through the host;

3And they commanded the people, saying, When ye see the ark of the covenant of the LORD your God, and the priests the Levites bearing it, then ye shall remove from your place, and go after it.

4Yet there shall be a space between you and it, about two thousand cubits by measure: come not near unto it, that ye may know the way by which ye must go: for ye have not passed this way heretofore.

5And Joshua said unto the people, Sanctify yourselves: for to morrow the LORD will do wonders among you.

6And Joshua spake unto the priests, saying, Take up the ark of the covenant, and pass over before the people. And they took up the ark of the covenant, and went before the people.

7And the LORD said unto Joshua, This day will I begin to magnify thee in the sight of all Israel, that they may know that, as I was with Moses, so I will be with thee.

8And thou shalt command the priests that bear the ark of the covenant, saying, When ye are come to the brink of the water of Jordan, ye shall stand still in Jordan.

9And Joshua said unto the children of Israel, Come hither, and hear the words of the LORD your God.

10And Joshua said, Hereby ye shall know that the living God is among you, and that he will without fail drive out from before you the Canaanites, and the Hittites, and the Hivites, and the Perizzites, and the Girgashites, and the Amorites, and the Jebusites.

11Behold, the ark of the covenant of the LORD of all the earth passeth over before you into Jordan.

12Now therefore take you twelve men out of the tribes of Israel, out of every tribe a man.

13And it shall come to pass, as soon as the soles of the feet of the priests that bear the ark of the LORD, the LORD of all the earth, shall rest in the waters of Jordan, that the waters of Jordan shall be cut off from the waters that come down from above; and they shall stand upon an heap.

14And it came to pass, when the people removed from their tents, to pass over Jordan, and the priests bearing the ark of the covenant before the people;
15And as they that bare the ark were come unto Jordan, and the feet of the priests that bare the ark were dipped in the brim of the water, (for Jordan overfloweth all his banks all the time of harvest,)
16That the waters which came down from above stood and rose up upon an heap very far from the city Adam, that is beside Zaretan: and those that came down toward the sea of the plain, even the salt sea, failed, and were cut off: and the people passed over right against Jericho.
17And the priests that bare the ark of the covenant of the LORD stood firm on dry ground in the midst of Jordan, and all the Israelites passed over on dry ground, until all the people were passed clean over Jordan.

JOSHUA 4

1And it came to pass, when all the people were clean passed over Jordan, that the LORD spake unto Joshua, saying,
2Take you twelve men out of the people, out of every tribe a man,
3And command ye them, saying, Take you hence out of the midst of Jordan, out of the place where the priests' feet stood firm, twelve stones, and ye shall carry them over with you, and leave them in the lodging place, where ye shall lodge this night.
4Then Joshua called the twelve men, whom he had prepared of the children of Israel, out of every tribe a man:
5And Joshua said unto them, Pass over before the ark of the LORD your God into the midst of Jordan, and take you up every man of you a stone upon his shoulder, according unto the number of the tribes of the children of Israel:
6That this may be a sign among you, that when your children ask their fathers in time to come, saying, What mean ye by these stones?
7Then ye shall answer them, That the waters of Jordan were cut off before the ark of the covenant of the LORD; when it passed

over Jordan, the waters of Jordan were cut off: and these stones shall be for a memorial unto the children of Israel for ever.

8 And the children of Israel did so as Joshua commanded, and took up twelve stones out of the midst of Jordan, as the LORD spake unto Joshua, according to the number of the tribes of the children of Israel, and carried them over with them unto the place where they lodged, and laid them down there.

9 And Joshua set up twelve stones in the midst of Jordan, in the place where the feet of the priests which bare the ark of the covenant stood: and they are there unto this day.

10 For the priests which bare the ark stood in the midst of Jordan, until everything was finished that the LORD commanded Joshua to speak unto the people, according to all that Moses commanded Joshua: and the people hasted and passed over.

11 And it came to pass, when all the people were clean passed over, that the ark of the LORD passed over, and the priests, in the presence of the people.

12 And the children of Reuben, and the children of Gad, and half the tribe of Manasseh, passed over armed before the children of Israel, as Moses spake unto them:

13 About forty thousand prepared for war passed over before the LORD unto battle, to the plains of Jericho.

14 On that day the LORD magnified Joshua in the sight of all Israel; and they feared him, as they feared Moses, all the days of his life.

15 And the LORD spake unto Joshua, saying,

16 Command the priests that bear the ark of the testimony, that they come up out of Jordan.

17 Joshua therefore commanded the priests, saying, Come ye up out of Jordan.

18 And it came to pass, when the priests that bare the ark of the covenant of the LORD were come up out of the midst of Jordan, and the soles of the priests' feet were lifted up unto the dry land, that the waters of Jordan returned unto their place, and flowed over all his banks, as they did before.

19 And the people came up out of Jordan on the tenth day of the first month, and encamped in Gilgal, in the east border of Jericho.

20And those twelve stones, which they took out of Jordan, did Joshua pitch in Gilgal.
21And he spake unto the children of Israel, saying, When your children shall ask their fathers in time to come, saying, What mean these stones?
22Then ye shall let your children know, saying, Israel came over this Jordan on dry land.
23For the LORD your God dried up the waters of Jordan from before you, until ye were passed over, as the LORD your God did to the Red sea, which he dried up from before us, until we were gone over:
24That all the people of the earth might know the hand of the LORD, that it is mighty: that ye might fear the LORD your God for ever.

PSALM 23

1The LORD is my shepherd; I shall not want.
2He maketh me to lie down in green pastures: he leadeth me beside the still waters.
3He restoreth my soul: he leadeth me in the paths of righteousness for his name's sake.
4Yea, though I walk through the valley of the shadow of death, I will fear no evil: for thou art with me; thy rod and thy staff they comfort me.
5Thou preparest a table before me in the presence of mine enemies: thou anointest my head with oil; my cup runneth over.
6Surely goodness and mercy shall follow me all the days of my life: and I will dwell in the house of the LORD for ever.

PSALM 149:3

Let them praise his name in the dance: let them sing praises unto him with the timbrel and harp.

PSALM 150:3-4

3Praise him with the sound of the trumpet: praise him with the psaltery and harp.
4Praise him with the timbrel and dance: praise him with stringed instruments and organs.

PROVERBS 24:16
For a just man falleth seven times, and riseth up again: but the wicked shall fall into mischief.

LAMENTATIONS 3:22-23
22It is of the LORD's mercies that we are not consumed, because his compassions fail not.
23They are new every morning: great is thy faithfulness

LUKE 12:48
But he that knew not, and did commit things worthy of stripes, shall be beaten with few stripes. For unto whomsoever much is given, of him shall be much required: and to whom men have committed much, of him they will ask the more

ROMANS 8:27
And he that searcheth the hearts knoweth what is the mind of the Spirit, because he maketh intercession for the saints according to the will of God.

ROMANS 8:36
As it is written, For thy sake we are killed all the day long; we are accounted as sheep for the slaughter

1 CORINTHIANS 2:14
But the natural man receiveth not the things of the Spirit of God: for they are foolishness unto him: neither can he know them, because they are spiritually discerned.

2 CORINTHIANS 12:9
And he said unto me, My grace is sufficient for thee: for my strength is made perfect in weakness. Most gladly therefore will I rather glory in my infirmities, that the power of Christ may rest upon me.

1 JOHN 4:4
Ye are of God, little children, and have overcome them: because greater is he that is in you, than he that is in the world.